AID TO

Third Edition

by

Roy Bryan

WYOMING · 2001

AID TO PATROL LEADERSHIP

by

ROY BRYAN

CORINTHIAN ENTERPRISE COMPANY
WYOMING, UNITED STATES OF AMERICA

BIBLIOGRAPHICAL NOTE

FIRST EDITION: *January, 1997.*

SECOND EDITION: © *and printed 1997.*

THIRD EDITION: © *1998.*
First printing, 2001.

ISBN 0 - 9711543 - 0 - 9

A patrol leader

FOREWORD

Being a patrol leader gives you authority over your patrol. With authority always comes responsibility; the two are inseparable. It is hoped that this book will aid you, and through you – your patrol, to serve God, your country, and other people better, and to have fun doing it.

ACKNOWLEDGEMENTS

I am grateful to Troop 777, Central Wyoming Council, Boy Scouts of America, for allowing me to work with them as assistant scoutmaster (1996-1998) and now as scoutmaster, and further for allowing me the liberty of writing this book for their patrol leaders. The previous scoutmaster, Mr. Jim Jones, also needs to be thanked for over-reading the first draft of this book (first edition).

I would like to thank the five Scouts and five adults who read and evaluated the draft of the second edition – I appreciated your input. They are: (Scouts:) Ryan Andrews, Ryan Bench, Stuart Cooper, Scott Hunter, Daniel Williamson; (adults:) Al Allen, Howard Andrews, Jim Crouch, James Porter, and Dave Tenney. I would like to thank Dave Tenney a second time for his help with the "Patrol Method" portion of our troop's Scout Officer Training Course, from which comes Chapter III of this book.

Lastly, the Frontiersman patrol of Troop 144, Central Wyoming Council, Boy Scouts of America, needs to be thanked for allowing me to be their patrol leader for three or more years, providing me with invaluable experience at the job.

INTRODUCTION AND APOLOGIES

If you are a Scout looking at this book for the first time, I would recommend skipping this stuff and going to Chapter I.

Let me begin by saying that I am amazed at the success of Aid to Patrol Leadership! The book began as a small, local project for the troop, and has had such a big response that the leadership in the troop is being excessively burdened by the work associated with such a large volume of book handling. At a recent troop committee meeting, we decided that we are a Scout troop, not a publishing and shipping company.

I was pleased when a publishing company offered to take over the publication and distribution of this book. Troop 777, Central Wyoming Council, Boy Scouts of America, will continue to receive all royalties from the sale of these books so long as the troop continues to exist. On behalf of our oft ailing troop bank account, I would like to thank you for purchasing this book.

Aid to Patrol Leadership began in January of 1997. I joined the troop only a month or two prior as assistant scoutmaster, after being out of Scouting for ten years or so. We began reorganizing and recruiting to prevent the demise of a dying troop. After recruiting a patrol of all new Scouts, I volunteered to buy the newly elected patrol leaders and their assistants a copy of the Official Patrol Leaders' Handbook so that they would have something to help them understand their job. When I called to the council office to see if they had any, the trading post manager said he did not have any. Elections were only a week away; could he order some and have them in only a week? He checked. The Patrol Leaders' Handbook was not listed in his catalogue. He concluded that they must not have it available anymore.

The BSA not have a Patrol Leaders' Handbook??? What had happened in Scouting in the ten years I was away??? So, rather than give up, I looked at a copy of the <u>Official Patrol Leaders' Handbook</u> out of the 1970's, drew on my own experiences as patrol leader, and quickly wrote a book (more like a pamphlet) in a week's time. This was the 1st edition of <u>Aid to Patrol Leadership.</u> It was printed on a typewriter, had no pictures, few stories, and plenty of errors. (Fortunately, only ten copies were printed.)

I apologized for the poor quality of the 1st edition, and told them I would take more time and rewrite it. (I called it the "1st edition" to reminded myself of its inadequacies and be sure to fix them in a 2nd edition.) In the process of researching for the 2nd edition, I happened to talk with my friendly local district executive. When I expressed my amazement at the discontinuance of the BSA's <u>Patrol Leaders' Handbook</u>, he informed me that it had not been discontinued, but the name had been changed to the <u>Junior Leader Handbook</u>! So I wrote my book for nothing!

When I was contemplating dropping the whole project, several of the people who had read the 1st edition (especially Scouts) said it was good, and I really should finish my revision. In addition, when the district executive heard that I was going to a Wood Badge course that summer, he recommended that I stop working on the book until after Wood Badge – he said it would make a great ticket item.

The draft of the 2nd edition was reviewed by five Scouts and five adult Scouters, and many of their suggestions were incorporated into the book. <u>Aid to Patrol Leadership</u>, 2nd edition, was finished and copyrighted in September, 1997. I spent the next several months reading rejection letters from various publishing companies.

Endeavor Books, a book printing company here in Casper, Wyoming, agreed to print 150 copies of the book. These were delivered and the whole lot sold in short order. And the orders kept coming and coming! The offer of publication came at the right time, since this was more than the troop bargained for!

With reprinting/publication comes the luxury of a 3rd edition. The chapter on the Patrol Method is an adapted excerpt from our troop's Scout Officer Training Course (troop JLT), and I would like to thank Mr. Dave Tenney for his help with this material. Other parts of the book were touched up, and small sections added here and there. The illustrations received much needed attention as well.

This brings us to the "apologies." I am a person who likes to have all of the facts and details correct, and the 2nd edition contains some errors and shortcomings. (Hence another reason for the 3rd edition.) I was dismayed to find that the words "east" and "west" were transposed in the story of the Boers' final attack on Mafeking (Chapter I). In addition, I found out later that there were more than two whites supervising the native levy in the Ashanti Campaign (Chapter V of the 2nd ed., Chapter VI in the 3rd ed.).

The bugle calls (Appendix D) were not free of errors, either. The one entitled "Boots and Saddles" is not really called that, and is a less common version of a Civil War bugle call to pack up camp. I am still not sure what its real name is ("The General"?), and I should not have included it. Several typos also slipped through, and I have no one to blame but myself – I typed the whole thing.

I need to also apologize for the less than professional illustrations in the book (both 2nd and 3rd editions). I am the artist for them all, and thus have no one to hide behind. I often find it easier to just draw what is on my mind rather than try to find the perfect picture to put in. So I did.

Lastly, I apologize for the author. There are those who are far more qualified than myself to write this book. My experiences at leadership stem mainly from Boy Scouting and from my work as an emergency room physician. My information about Scouts comes from Baden-Powell's works, the Boy Scouts of America, and from books about Baden-Powell and Boy Scouting (see bibliography). But most importantly, the Bible is my principle source for how to conduct oneself as a leader, and as a gentleman. I recommend that the reader consult this last work, and its Author, for further and better information on the subject.

Respectfully,

Roy Bryan MD, SM
(Wyoming – August, 1998)

P.S. – Incidentally, English was my weakest subject in high school and college!

Addendum

A large number of people have been waiting for this book for a long time. By the Spring of 2000 the book still had not been published, and the contract with the publisher was cancelled. An alternative publisher was sought and secured.

With Sincerest Apologies,

Roy Bryan MD, LSC
(Botswana, Africa – April, 2000)

Second Addendum

Here we are one year later and the second publisher has been moving so slowly that it is in danger of being overrun by a glacier. I consider myself to be a man of action, and all of this inactivity is quite frustrating and eye opening to me. So, I will try yet another route…

With Final Apologies,

Roy Bryan, MD, ASM
(Wyoming – May, 2001)

TABLE OF CONTENTS

CHAPTER I : ACTION 1
Do Something!

CHAPTER II : THE PATROL 13
What is a Patrol? Patrol Name and Identity. Patrol Spirit. The Patrol in Action. The Patrol on Campouts. Strengthening the Patrol.

CHAPTER III : THE PATROL METHOD 27
Patrols. Training the New Recruits. Brownsea. Independence, Loyalty, Respect, and Obedience. The Three-fold Cord. Summary.

CHAPTER IV : THE PATROL LEADER 37
Emblem. Authority Structure of the Boy Scouts of America. Patrol Leader Selection. Patrol Leader Character. Patrol Leader Responsibilities. Appointing an Assistant Patrol Leader. The Acting Patrol Leader. Your Successor.

CHAPTER V : THE ASSISTANT PATROL LEADER 51
Emblem. Assistant Patrol Leader Selection. How to Assist. Assistant Patrol Leader Character. Assistant Patrol Leader Responsibilities.

CHAPTER VI : LEADERSHIP 57
How to be a Leader. Leading by Example. Leading by Criticism. Leading by Telling People What To Do. Leading by Being the Captain. Leading by Delegation of Responsibility. Leading by Organization and Preparation. Conflicts and Problems. Success. Failure. Pain and Guilt. Unpleasant Tasks.

CHAPTER VII : PATROL MEETINGS AND ACTIVITIES 77
Patrol Meetings. Patrol Activities. Who to Invite to a Patrol Meeting. But I Can't Do It.

CHAPTER VIII : PATROL MEMBERSHIP 81
Getting New Members. Losing Members. Getting Rid of Members.

CHAPTER IX : PATROL RECORDS 87
Why Keep Records? Who Keeps the Records? Patrol Membership Records. Patrol Activity Records. Patrol Finance Records.

CHAPTER X : DISBANDING THE PATROL   91

THE BOY IS THERE NO MORE   95

AUTHOR'S PATROLS   97

BIBLIOGRAPHY   99

APPENDIX A : PATROL PATCHES (AND NAMES)
    AVAILABLE FROM THE BSA, 1998   101

APPENDIX B : BADEN-POWELL PATROL
    REQUIREMENTS   103

APPENDIX C : SOME COMMON ABBREVIATIONS…   105

APPENDIX D : CAMP BUGLE CALLS   107

AID TO PATROL LEADERSHIP

Third Edition

Roy Bryan

CHAPTER I

ACTION

By August of 1914 Europe was on the edge of war. The assassination of the Austrian Archduke Franz Ferdinand had plunged Germany into war with Russia and France. The British were not at war, but they might be involved soon.

In the Mediterranean Sea was the German battlecruiser GOEBEN. It was a large, modern type of ship designed with the firepower of a battleship and the speed (and light armour) of a cruiser. It could outfight anything that was as fast as itself and could outrun anything more powerful. This made it a perfect surface raider. Surface raiders are ships that go around sinking enemy cargo ships and smaller warships, and avoiding combat with big enemy ships. This not only sinks ships, but causes panic in an area and interrupts trade and supply. It was because of the GOEBEN that French troop transports in North Africa were afraid to leave for France until they could be escorted safely by the big ships of the French Navy.

The German ships in the Mediterranean were under the command of Admiral Wilhelm Souchon, who flew his flag aboard the GOEBEN. He and the GOEBEN left the Adriatic Sea, rendezvoused with the German light cruiser BRESLAU, and put in to the Italian port of Messina, on the island of Sicily, on August 2. There they took on coal.

Although not at war, the British knew that they could be at war with the Germans very soon (and they were three days later). British Admiral Sir Christopher Berkeley Milne was in command of the British Mediterranean Fleet, and he set about preparing for war. He *gathered his ships in Malta. He had three battlecruisers, the* INFLEXIBLE, INDOMITABLE, *and* INDEFATIGABLE, *four armoured cruisers, the* DEFENCE, DUKE OF EDINBURGH, WARRIOR *and* BLACK PRINCE, *and many light cruisers and destroyers. He had two primary jobs: to find the* GOEBEN *and keep track of it, so that if war did come he could destroy her quickly, and to block the Strait of Otranto, keeping the Austrian fleet from entering the eastern Mediterranean. He at first sent the battlecruisers* INDOMITABLE *and* INDEFATIGABLE, *and all of the armoured cruisers, to guard the Adriatic Sea and the*

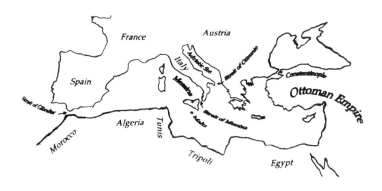

The Mediterranean Sea

Strait of Otranto, but when he found out on August 3 that the GOEBEN *and* BRESLAU *had disappeared from Messina, he called the two battlecruisers back westward to look for them.*

On the evening of August 3, Germany and France were officially at war. The French sent their battlefleet southward to protect their colony of Algeria. On the morning of August 4, before the French battlefleet could arrive, the GOEBEN *and* BRESLAU *appeared off of Algeria and began shelling two of the towns there.*

S.M.S. GOEBEN under full steam. She billowed thick black smoke when being pursued in the Mediterranean because of the poor quality coal taken on in Messina.

They then disappeared just as fast as they had appeared, but at least Admiral Milne and the French knew that the German ships were somewhere in the western Mediterranean. The French steamed westward, thinking that the Germans may try to sail through the Strait of Gibralter and out into the Atlantic. The British INDOMITABLE *and* INDEFATIGABLE *covered their escape route to the east.*

At 9:30 in the morning of August 4, the British found the German ships escaping to the east. The British had the Germans at an advantage of two battlecruisers to one, and the British wanted to fight. But they were not at war! Even though the Germans and French were already fighting, war had not been declared between Germany and Britain. The British ships could not attack.

The INDOMITABLE *and* INDEFATIGABLE *began following the German ships, thinking that as soon as they heard on the radio that* war had been declared they would start shooting. They followed the GOEBEN and BRESLAU all day, but as night fell the German ships disappeared in a fog. At midnight, only three hours after the British lost contact with the Germans in the fog, war was officially declared between England and Germany.

Admiral Milne received word that the German ships he was hunting for (and had just lost) had returned to Messina. However, since this was an Italian port, and Italy had declared herself neutral in the war, there could be no fighting within six miles of the Italian coast, and this included the Strait of Messina. Admiral Milne personally took his flagship, the battlecruiser INFLEXIBLE, and joined the other two battlecruisers on the west side. (The INDOMITABLE had to leave to coal, so this cut him down to only two battlecruisers again.) He thought that Admiral Souchon would probably have another run at the French Algerian coast, or some other place in the western Mediterranean, so he concentrated his force westward. In case the Germans did try to escape into the eastern Mediterranean, he stationed the light cruiser GLOUCESTER all by herself on the east side of the Strait of Messina. Which way would the Germans go?

Near sunset on August 6 the Germans left Messina, and they steamed east. The GLOUCESTER found the GOEBEN and BRESLAU and followed them, but she stayed well away from the two ships for fear of being ripped to shreds by the GOEBEN's 11.1 inch guns. The GLOUCESTER's radio kept the British informed of where the German ships were, and the Germans continued eastward. The Germans shifted course, and tried other tricks to lose the GLOUCESTER, but the GLOUCESTER hung on and refused to be tricked or driven away.

Although Admiral Milne's battlecruisers were too far away for him to catch up, the four armoured cruisers sent to guard the Strait of Otranto from the Austrians were in a good position to intercept the GOEBEN and BRESLAU. Admiral Troubridge, commanding this British squadron, headed toward the GOEBEN and BRESLAU to intercept. The GLOUCESTER kept him informed of where the German ships were.

On August 7, before dawn, as the DEFENCE, BLACK PRINCE, WARRIOR *and* DUKE OF EDINBURGH, *and their eight destroyers, were racing southward to attack Admiral Souchon's ships, Admiral Troubridge began to think about what he was heading into. Not only were the* GOEBEN'S *11.1 inch guns bigger and of longer range than the 9.2 inch guns on his armoured cruisers, but the* GOEBEN *was faster than his ships. He might very well get into big trouble, and he would not be able to escape if he did start to lose. In addition, he had received orders not to attack a "superior force," and the* GOEBEN'S *11.1 inch guns were certainly superior to what he had to fight with. Just before dawn he decided it would be too dangerous to try and attack the* GOEBEN, *so he turned all of his ships around!*

H.M.S. GLOUCESTER, *the dwarf that shadowed the giant.*

The GOEBEN and BRESLAU escaped unchallenged and later put into the Turkish port of Constantinople. The arrival of such a powerful German ship impressed the Turks, and eventually paved the way for the Ottoman Empire to enter the war on Germany's side. The GOEBEN and BRESLAU were later sold to the Turks and renamed YAVUS SULTAN SELIM and MIDILLIE.

Because he had turned around and not attacked the German ships, British Admiral Troubridge was brought before a court martial in November of 1914, but he was acquitted. However, because of the way the Royal Navy felt about his actions, he was never again given a sea command, and he eventually retired in disgrace.

Fifteen years earlier, in the Fall of 1899, tensions were rising between the British and the Boers[1] in South Africa, and war seemed imminent. Colonel R. S. S. Baden-Powell had been sent to organize British defenses to the north and east of the Boers, in the area of Rhodesia and the Bechuanaland Protectorate (modern day Zimbabwe and Botswana). He divided his command between Rhodesia and Bechuanaland, and he himself commanded the Bechuanaland area.

He was short on men and supplies, but still managed to organize two regiments of volunteers. He chose to base his defense out of the town of Mafeking, because it was along the railway that led from Cape Town up toward Rhodesia, and because the Boers would most likely consider the taking of Mafeking a top priority. He was right.

---

[1] The Boers are white descendants of Dutch settlers in southern Africa. When the British were given the southern portion of Africa, the Boers moved northward to avoid the British and remain independent. They formed two autonomous areas: the Transvaal and the Orange Free State. During the Boer War of 1899-1902, these areas were conquered by the British and are today part of the country of South Africa.

As jy die lyn kan lees dan weet jy dalk meer van die Afrikaner geschiedenis as ek.

Colonel R. S. S. Baden-Powell

He had spent a considerable amount of time building fortifications around the town and coming up with ways to make the Boers think he was better defended than he was. They used dynamite to create a phony minefield around the town, and put steel rails on the side of a railroad engine to make an armoured train. They put in artillery positions on the heights and dug defensive trenches. In short, they did whatever they could think of to get ready.

In October, when war did come, Colonel Baden-Powell and his men soon found themselves surrounded in Mafeking, and outnumbered nine to one. To make matters worse, the Boers had sent General Cronje, "The Lion of the Transvaal," to personally make sure that Mafeking was taken quickly. Things looked grim for Mafeking.

Colonel Baden-Powell knew that it was going to be hard to hold on. He began by encouraging his men and the townspeople, and by issuing some standing orders to his men. Among the orders was this: "Don't be afraid to act for fear of making a mistake – 'a man who never made a mistake never made anything.'"[2] He wanted his men to be bold and courageous. He knew if they were not then the Boers would easily roll right over them.

---

[2]From the standing orders given by Colonel Baden-Powell at the beginning of the Boer War. Baden-Powell attributes this quote to Napoleon.

*Boer men and boys in the trenches around Mafeking.
Since most Boers were farmers and ranchers, they learned horsemanship and
marksmanship early, and they could live and move in the veld with little difficulty.
Although the Boers were poorly organized by military standards, their upbringing
made each individual boy and man quite a formidable soldier when the time came.*

Colonel Baden-Powell hoped to sting the Boers that had surrounded him before they had a chance to attack the town. Early in the morning of October 14 he received word that there was a strong party of Boers approaching from the north. He sent out his armoured train and a good many of his men to surprise attack. The Boers were not expecting such an attack from the defenders and were driven back at first. When they did decide to fight, Colonel Baden-Powell sent out even more men to drive them back again. In so doing he risked the entire defense of Mafeking, since there were very few people left in the town to defend it. His boldness worked, though. The Boers retreated with far heavier losses than the British, and they had lost a good deal of confidence in their ability to overrun the British in Mafeking.

The Boers did not want to directly assault Mafeking after losing the opening battle, so they decided to simply shell Mafeking into submission. But the bombproof shelters that Baden-Powell had ordered dug into the town before the war made the shelling fairly useless. The bomb shelters worked so well that, after the first bombardment or two, Baden-Powell sent a message to his superiors, saying: "All well. Four hours' bombardment. One dog killed."

Next the Boers decided to dig trenches toward Mafeking. This was going well until the British surprise attacked the workers in the trenches one night. After that the Boers were very slow and afraid to work much farther on the trenches. To discourage them even further, Baden-Powell staged several fake night attacks on the trenches, which caused the Boers to shoot at each other.

Finally, on the 31st of October, the Boers decided to make a frontal attack on one of the hills overlooking the town. If they could get control of this hill, they could shell and even shoot into Mafeking much more easily. The attack began with the shelling of the hill, and the British left the hill until the shelling stopped. Then, as the Boers approached the hill from three sides, the British went back up onto the hill to fire down on the Boers. Not being content with this, Colonel Baden-Powell sent his men out to flank the Boers on bothsides. The Boers became caught in a crossfire and began to hesitate in their advance. Even though the Boer officers tried to urge them on, the Boer soldiers finally broke and ran. Once again, Baden-Powell's strategy had driven off a larger force.

Finally General Cronje decided he was wasting his time attacking Mafeking and thought he might starve it into submission. General Cronje took most of the Boers and went elsewhere where he could do more good. Mafeking was still surrounded and outnumbered two to one, but it was still under British control. For months the people in Mafeking had to endure daily bombardments and food rationing.

The day after Christmas Colonel Baden-Powell launched a surprise attack on one of the Boer gun positions. Everything seemed to go wrong with the attack, and many brave British officers and men were killed without accomplishing anything. Baden-Powell later found out that a spy had warned the Boers ahead of time about the attack, and the Boers had set a trap.

For the next several months the Boers bombed Mafeking, and the British went hungry and endured it. After his loss at Christmas time he was hesitant to risk another attack that would weaken his forces even more.

Colonel Baden-Powell frequently sent out men to spy on the enemy camps. He himself even went out to spy on different occasions so he could see the Boer positions first hand.

Runners would sneak through the Boer lines periodically and bring news of how the war was going. Many times the news was bad. Colonel Baden-Powell sent messages out by these runners to keep his superiors informed of the happenings in Mafeking, but he himself stayed in Mafeking.

By the spring of 1900 the British began to push the Boers back all over South Africa. The other towns in South Africa that were under siege, Ladysmith and Kimberly, were relieved; Mafeking became the last one to still be encircled by the Boers. Previous attempts to break the siege there had failed, but in May the British approached again. The Boers made one final attempt to take Mafeking.

On May 12, 1900, the Boers surprised the British in Mafeking with a night attack from the east and the west. They broke through the defenses on the west side of town and began burning native huts as a signal for the Boers on the east to press the attack. It appeared that Mafeking might fall after all.

Colonel Baden-Powell thought quickly. He sent a message indicating that the Boers who had broken in from the west were surrounded in the middle of town and were about to surrender. When the Boers attacking from the east heard this, they decided the attack must have failed, so they went back to their camp. This gave Baden-Powell the break he needed. He closed the hole in his defenses in the west, and then surrounded the Boers that had entered Mafeking. They surrendered.

Five days later, British forces attacking Mafeking from the west managed to defeat the Boers surrounding Mafeking and drive them off. After 217 days, the siege of Mafeking was over. British in Mafeking were elated to be free again and happy to have food!

Colonel Baden-Powell had become well known in England during the siege, and he became an instant national hero. He was immediately promoted two ranks to Major-General, and eventually became the Inspector-General of all British cavalry throughout the British Empire. He retired from the military in 1910 to devote full time to a project of his: Boy Scouts.

These two officers, Admiral Troubridge and Colonel Baden-Powell, were both placed in situations where the odds were against them. The first thought that if he did nothing then nothing bad would happen. The second thought that if he didn't do something then something bad would happen to him and his men. One came out a hero, the other lost his career. Which are you?

DO SOMETHING!

Being a patrol leader (or an assistant patrol leader) is an honor. It is also an opportunity. Some of the opportunities will just happen to you, but many of the opportunities you can make happen.

Instead of being mediocre, strive to be the best, most outstanding leader you can be. Encourage your patrol to be the best that it can be. The more you and your patrol do, the more experiences you will have, the more you will learn, and the more fun you will have. Be inventive! Be creative! Take pride in how well you and your patrol are doing. The more you do and know, the more there is to be proud of.

If your patrol does well, then you will get the credit. If your patrol does poorly, then you will get the blame. You will look much better if they do well, so encourage them to do the best that they can, and you do the same.

As a patrol leader (or an assistant patrol leader) you have been given an opportunity to be awesome, or to be bland. In a world which increasingly wants to sit back and be entertained, and which wants to take more and more and give less and less, I challenge you to be the opposite. I challenge you to throw yourself wholeheartedly into your leadership position and do something great with it!

CHAPTER II

THE PATROL

During the dark morning hours of March 9, 1916, about 500 Mexicans, led by Francisco Pancho Villa, crossed the border near Columbus, New Mexico, and proceeded to attack the town, its inhabitants, and the cavalry stationed there. Seventeen Americans were killed, more civilians than soldiers, and the Mexican rebels were driven away and pursued into Mexico by a vastly outnumbered U.S. cavalry detachment. Mexico was involved in a civil war and was powerless to stop such rebel incursions into the United States. But the U.S. government was going to make sure that this stopped, and that the people responsible paid.

On March 15, 1916, Brigadier General John J. Pershing led four U.S. cavalry regiments and two U.S. infantry regiments as they began to cross the border into Mexico. His task was to capture Villa and to disperse his bandits. The Mexican government had initially given permission for the Americans to enter, but retracted permission almost immediately, so that General Pershing was entering Mexico against the will of the Mexican government. American President Wilson assured the Mexicans that his forces would leave as soon as Villa was captured.

For three months the American Punitive Expedition drove deeper and deeper into Mexico, attacking Pancho Villa's men wherever they found them. Several of Villa's commanders were captured or killed, and Villa's rebels were being dispersed everywhere. Villa narrowly escaped capture several times, and then seemed to disappear.[1]

The Mexican people generally resented the U.S. intrusion, and many did their best to cause problems for Pershing's men. The desert areas of northern Mexico were tough on men and horses alike, making the campaign all the more challenging. In addition, the political maneuvering between Washington and Mexico City was becoming more difficult the deeper Pershing drove into Mexico, and if something bad happened, a full scale war could result.

Something bad did happen, on June 21st. Near the town of Carrizal, two troops of scouting U.S. cavalry met with a superior number of Mexican government troops. The governmental Mexican troops refused to let the Americans pass through Carrizal, and a stubborn American cavalry captain insisted that they would. The Americans charged and were cut down by the Mexicans. Most of the cavalrymen were killed or captured, only a few escaped.

With such a vicious fight between American and Mexican government troops, a war seemed just around the corner. The Mexican president was involved in a civil war, and he could not back down against the unpopular Americans or his country would see him as weak against the Americans. This would strengthen the Mexican rebels. President Wilson was facing an election in a few months and the race was going to be close. If he backed down with Mexico, he would likely lose the election. Although neither side really wanted a war with the other, neither government was in a position to stop one.

The two governments decided to try and negotiate. The negotiations went poorly, since neither president was willing to back down. Negotiations continued for six months or more.

---

[1] As it turned out, Villa had been accidentally shot in the leg by one of his own men early in the campaign. Most of the time that the Americans were looking for him he and two of his men were out in the desert, in a cave. Villa nearly died from the infection in his leg. He did survive, but it took him a long time to recover, and even longer to reassemble his men after they had been hunted down or dispersed by the advancing Americans.

John J. Pershing as a Major General during the Mexican Campaign

In the meantime, President Wilson ordered General Pershing to stop where he was. If he moved forward, there might be another fight, and a war would probably result if there was another fight. If Pershing moved back, it would look like the Americans had been beaten, and President Wilson needed all of the leverage available in the negotiations. So for months and months, General Pershing could do nothing with his troops but sit in the middle of a hostile Mexico.

But he did not simply do nothing. If he could not move his main troops, he could still send out patrols. Soon patrols were doing all of the work. The patrols continued the hunt for Villa and his men. The patrols kept track of Mexican government troop movements and gave valuable information to General Pershing. The patrols protected the long, exposed supply lines, and patrolled the areas around the American camps to keep them safe. Patrols would be sent out into the field to do whatever job needed to be done, including training. Some patrols were on horseback, others on foot. Some of the patrols were even in a brand new invention: the airplane. The patrols became the only way that General Pershing could do anything.

By September, Villa and his men were back. They avoided the American troops, which Villa knew could not move, and began attacking Mexican government troops. The Mexican troops were being defeated, and Villa was becoming stronger. Villa vowed a war with America if he was made leader of Mexico. As he became stronger and more active, the tension between the U.S. and Mexico got even worse. Negotiations went nowhere.

Finally in January, 1917, the Mexican government won a large victory over Villa and his men. Even though Villa escaped, he did not have enough men left to cause any harm. President Wilson took advantage of the situation and declared the emergency over. He ordered the Americans to leave Mexico.

General Pershing went on to become the commander of the American Expeditionary Force in Europe, when the United States entered World War I later in the same year. Francisco Pancho Villa continued to be an outlaw in Mexico until he decided in 1920 that he had had enough. He agreed to stop fighting the Mexican government in exchange for amnesty and a nice ranch in northern Mexico. He lived on his ranch for a few years and survived several assassination attempts. But finally, in 1923, he and a car load of his friends were gunned down by someone that owed him money.

For most of Pershing's time in Mexico, it was his patrols that did the work.

WHAT IS A PATROL?

A patrol is any small group of men or boys who are out in the field for a specific purpose. The purpose may be to scout out enemy positions, protect their own position, explore an area, practice, train themselves, or do just about anything else. Sometimes a patrol's task is exciting; sometimes it is boring.

In Boy Scouting, a patrol is a group of three to eight boys that works together, camps together, eats together, competes together, and learns together. The reason for this number of boys is that any more than this becomes difficult for a boy leader to handle, and any less than this is not a group. Ideally, a patrol will have five to eight boys.

PATROL NAME AND IDENTITY

A patrol needs to have a name so that others know what to call it. For example, there was a television show many years ago about an American patrol in World War II called the Rat Patrol. In Scouts, the patrols are usually (but not always) named after animals. A list of all of the Boy Scouts of America patrol patches, and thus the names of patrols that you can buy patches for, is found in Appendix A of this book.

Each patrol member's uniform will have his patrol patch on the right sleeve, directly underneath the American flag.

The patrol will also have its own patrol flag, which should have the emblem of the patrol on it. For example, the Eagle Patrol would have an eagle on their patrol flag. The patrol is responsible for making their own flag and taking care of it. During troop meetings the patrol will line up behind their flag when the troop is in formation. On campouts the patrol flag will be flying proudly at the patrol campsite.

The patrol will also have a patrol yell, and/or a patrol call, that they make up themselves. The patrol yell is meant to show enthusiasm for the patrol. An example of a patrol yell for the Frontiersman patrol might be "Westward Ho!"

The patrol call is intended to allow patrol members to call to each other in the woods, or in the dark. For example, the raven patrol would make the sound of a raven. Other people hearing the call would think it is just the sound of a raven in the woods, and not know it is a patrol call. In Baden-Powell's original Scouting for Boys books, he said that no scout was allowed to use the call of any patrol but his own.

The patrol may also want to have a patrol symbol (whether it be a drawing of their patrol emblem or some other symbol) that they can write on pieces of paper or draw on the ground to mark that the patrol was involved in whatever the symbol is written on. In times past, some Scouts even put their patrol symbol after their names when they write their names.

Some patrols have made special neckerchiefs to wear with their uniforms. Other patrols have made special neckerchief slides to wear, identifying them as a member of their patrol. I saw one patrol that all wore special ropes around their waists as belts, one end of the rope having a loop and the other end having a stick or button to put through the loop and hold the belt on. When the patrol needed a rope, each member would remove his rope belt and they would hook all of the belts together to make the rope. What can you do to make your patrol unique?

Fox Patrol, pennant shaped flag.

Flaming Arrow Patrol, cavalry standard shaped flag.

Bison Patrol, square flag.

Flying Eagle Patrol, rectangular flag.

Examples of patrol flags

PATROL SPIRIT

The "patrol spirit" is difficult to define. The French call it the "esprit de corps,"[2] which is the friendship, loyalty, and enthusiasm shown by a group of people.

We want the patrol to have a good spirit. This means that the boys in the patrol get along well with each other and work well together as a group. It also means that they are enthusiastic and excited about what they are doing, whether it be a fun project, a boring project, a difficult project, an easy project, or simply waiting patiently for instructions.

Athos, Porthos, and Aramis: The Three Musketeers

Boys are active! If your patrol is not doing anything on its own then it is much less likely to appeal to the active nature of its members. One good way to boost the patrol spirit is to spend time together as a patrol doing things. If your patrol is doing things on its own, in addition to doing things with the troop, I wager that your patrol spirit will soar.

If the patrol is fun to be around, it probably has a good spirit. If it is not fun to be around it probably has a bad spirit. If it is active and accomplishing things then it probably has a good spirit. If it is not doing anything then it probably has a bad spirit, or at least a lazy spirit. If the members are excited

---

[2]This is pronounced like: "espree duh cor"

and enthusiastic, it probably has a good spirit. If they are always whining and complaining, it probably has a bad spirit. The better the patrol spirit, the funner the patrol is and the more the patrol will learn and accomplish.

The three musketeers had a saying that gave them a good spirit: "One for all and all for one!" Try this in your patrol and see how it works.

THE PATROL IN ACTION

The same Colonel Baden-Powell of Mafeking, when he was a Major and in command of a squadron of cavalry in the 13th Hussars[3] in Ireland, was involved in the summer military maneuvers of the British forces there. This is where army units practice their battlefield skills by dividing into two groups and "fighting" each other.

During the maneuvers, Baden-Powell was watching for an opportunity for his squadron to "attack" and capture an "enemy" artillery battery located on a hill. Unfortunately, there was a detachment of enemy cavalry defending the hill. The weather had been hot and dry, so that the movement of cavalry units was creating dust clouds that could easily be seen at a distance, and in the open hills of southern Ireland, one could see a good distance anyway. If he simply charged up to the hill, his squadron would surely be defeated.

He decided to take a chance on a wild idea. He took six of his men and tied ropes to their horses so that the ropes would drag behind the horses when they galloped. He then tied tree branches to the ropes, and sent the men riding off down a road that went near the hill. The dragging tree branches raised a large cloud of dust, and visible in the dust cloud was an occasional horse and rider.

---

[3](pronounced: huh-SAR) Hussars are light cavalry units. They are not used in modern armies because horse cavalry have been replaced by mechanized cavalry, namely tanks and other armoured vehicles.

As this decoy rode past the hill, the "enemy" cavalry thought surely this must be a whole squadron of cavalry, so they took off after them. With the defending cavalry out of the way, Major Baden-Powell and his squadron were able to ride up to the hill and capture it easily.

Shortly afterward a rider came up the hill and had Baden-Powell come with him. General Wolseley, commander of British forces in Ireland, had seen the trick and wanted to speak with the officer responsible. Since maneuvers were supposed to be an opportunity to practice established battlefield skills and not to pull stunts, Baden-Powell thought he might be in trouble. Instead, General Wolseley was quite impressed and said he liked to see officers who could think for themselves independent of the regulation book. General Wolseley later recommended Baden-Powell for several positions, including the one that led him to Mafeking.

The patrol does almost everything together in Boy Scouting. Patrols will usually compete against other patrols in competitions, showing their skills and practicing those skills at the same time. Patrols will cook together and camp together on campouts. Patrols will teach together, and learn together. They will help each other out, and even help out others as a patrol.

But the patrol is not a bunch of robots who sit around and wait for the scoutmaster or the adults to tell them everything to do. The founder of the Scouting movement, Robert S. S. Baden-Powell, was very clear that he did not want Scouts to be "soldiers" that were drilled in regimented thinking and action. Instead he wanted to teach boys to think for themselves and to be creative in their actions and their problem solving. Baden-Powell himself was often selected for responsibilities and promotions over other officers because he was very enthusiastic and creative in his leadership. These qualities should be encouraged in every member of the patrol.

For this reason, patrols are given a good deal of leeway in doing what they want to do. Patrols can go on patrol hikes or patrol campouts separate from troop activities.[4] They can plan activities for the patrol to do, and can even suggest activities for the troop to do. Patrols can arrange to learn about topics that interest the patrol, or can become experts on something that the patrol wants to do. The patrol might become specialists in compass work and navigation, or experts in first aid, or experts in radio communication or signaling, or whatever else they may choose. Patrols can have patrol meetings to discuss ideas and organize patrol activities. These can be during regular troop meetings (ask the scoutmaster for permission first) or at other times during the week.

A patrol practices signaling with a heliograph.

In short, an active patrol can do whatever projects or events that it wants to do.[4] The only limit to patrol activity is the enthusiasm and creativeness of the patrol members.

---

[4] All patrol activities need to have at lease one adult present, such as a parent. Also, the parents of all of the patrol members should know where their son is and what the activity will be.

THE PATROL ON CAMPOUTS

The patrol will cook and camp together on campouts. The patrol leader selects the campsite for the patrol and can arrange for the tents to be in some formation if he chooses. (For example, he may have all of the tents side by side with doors facing the same direction, or he may have the tents in a circle with all of the doors facing the campfire in the middle. He may also simply say "Camp in this area" and let the patrol members choose where to put their tents.)

The patrol flag should be flying to mark the patrol campsite. The cooking area and dining area will also be part of the patrol campsite, since the patrol cooks and eats together. (Several patrols may end up sharing the same cooking and dining areas, and the same campfire. Also, if there is a concern about bears, then the dining area is likely to be away from the patrol campsites.)

When on an outing, the patrol is responsible to make sure that none of its members become lost, and to notify the patrol leader if someone is missing. (The patrol leader will then notify the senior patrol leader or the scoutmaster.)

The patrol will also work together in the field. If a tower needs to be built, a dining fly needs to be set up, a signal needs to be sent, or a game is being played, the patrol accomplishes this as a group.

STRENGTHENING THE PATROL

The patrol members not only work together, but they grow because they work together. If the individual members of a patrol become stronger and better, then the patrol itself will become stronger and better. So, in addition to working on the spirit of the patrol (discussed earlier), the patrol should work on helping its individual members become better.

Patrol members can learn from each other. If one or more members are particularly good at something, have them teach the rest of the patrol. If no one in the patrol knows anything about the topic that the patrol wants to learn about, then assign someone to learn and then have him teach the rest of the patrol. Or, another way to do this is to go as a patrol to the scoutmaster (or other adult leader) and ask him to teach the patrol what the patrol wants to learn. (You will make your scoutmaster very proud of you if you approach him and ask him to teach you about something without him initiating it.) You can even earn merit badges as a patrol if you will contact the merit badge counselor and arrange something.

The patrol becomes stronger when its members teach each other and thus combine their knowledge and skills. Sometimes you will be the teacher and sometimes you will be the student. Accept both with humility, and the patrol will maintain its good spirit. If you know about something but are not invited to teach, don't take it personally. Instead, pay attention and be a good student; you may learn something about the subject that you did not know before. Try not to cause problems for the person who is teaching and try not to distract other members of the patrol who are learning.

If it falls on your shoulders to decide who will teach, try to choose someone who is interesting and knows his stuff. Also, try to have different people in the patrol teach each time, so that no one feels left out.

Sometimes a member of the patrol will act like he knows everything. He often will not want to learn, but will become upset if he is not always teaching. You may come to find out that this person does not know as much as he says he does. A person who does not want to learn because he already knows it all is a real hindrance to the patrol. You can get around many of your problems with him by having people outside of the patrol teach the patrol.

The Scoutmaster presenting a rank to a Scout at the Court of Honor

Another important aspect of strengthening the patrol is for each member to be advancing in rank. The ranks are designed to make sure that you are learning more and getting better, and if the scouts in your patrol are advancing in rank then they cannot help but to learn and to get better. The better the patrol members are, the better the patrol is. Encourage each other to move upward in rank toward Eagle, and congratulate scouts when they earn a new rank. Some patrol activities may be aimed specifically at accomplishing requirements for its members to move up in rank.

Baden-Powell once said, "A boy does not really get the value of the Scout training until he is a First-class Scout... I don't consider a boy is a real Scout till he has passed his first-class tests."[5] Are all of the members of your patrol First Class Scouts yet?

The Baden-Powell Patrol Award

Improving the good spirit in a patrol, having patrol members work together and learn together, and having patrol members advance in rank all will create a powerful patrol. Everyone will recognize a good patrol by the things it says and does. The BSA wants to recognize outstanding patrols with the Baden-Powell Patrol Award. This is a small patch with a star on it that is placed directly under the patrol patch on the scout's left sleeve. If you are interested in this award, a list of requirements is found in Appendix B.

---

[5] From B.- P.'s Outlook, pages 47 and 49.

CHAPTER III

THE PATROL METHOD

CAMP FIRE YARN.—No. 3.

BOY SCOUTS' ORGANISATION.

It is not intended that boy scouts should necessarily form a new corps separate from all others, but the boys who belong to any kind of existing organisation, such as schools, football clubs, Boys' or Church Lads' Brigades, factories, district messengers, Telegraph Service, Cadet Corps, etc., etc., can *also* take up scouting in addition to their other work or play—especially on Saturdays and Sundays.

But where there are any boys who do not belong to any kind of organisation—and there is a very large number of such boys about the United Kingdom—they can form themselves into Patrols and become Boy Scouts.

For this purpose officers are necessary.

> *Officers*: The head officer of all the boy scouts in the world is called the *Chief Scout*.
>
> *A Scout Master* is an officer who has charge of a troop. A troop consists of not less than three patrols. Scouts address the scout master as "Sir."
>
> *A Patrol Leader* is a scout appointed to command a patrol. A patrol consists of six scouts. Any lad or young man who learns scouting from this book can make himself a patrol leader and collect and train five or seven boys to be scouts.
>
> *A Corporal* is a scout selected by the patrol leader to be his assistant, and to take command of the patrol when he himself is away.

This is a reprint of page 35 of the original Boy Scout Handbook by Baden Powell, 1908.

There it is! The original organization and officer system for the Boy Scouts. Scouting was designed to be a program of boys lead by a boy leader – the patrol leader. He recruited his patrol and trained them as scouts. Several patrols made a troop, under the command of an adult leader – the scoutmaster. Councils, districts, troop committees, and all of that adult stuff were added later.

In the United States, another leadership position was created: the senior patrol leader (SPL). He is the boy officer in command of a troop. He answers to the scoutmaster.

The senior patrol leader appoints his own assistant – the assistant senior patrol leader (ASPL). This officer helps the senior patrol leader with his duties in the same way that the assistant patrol leader helps the patrol leader.

PATROLS

Why patrols? Why not just lump everyone together into a troop and let the scoutmaster lead? Other youth organizations have all adult leaders. Why doesn't Scouting do it that way? To answer that question, we must go back to the British Empire during the late Victorian Era (late 1800's)...

At one time, it was said that "The sun never sets on the British Empire." This meant that the British Empire was so large, and extended to so many corners of the globe, that it was always daytime in some part of the empire.

In order to maintain and defend this vast empire, the Royal Navy and the British Army were kept busy. Ships of the Royal Navy were stationed throughout the world, and the far flung colonies and stations of the empire were garrisoned by the British Army. Units were moved frequently, depending on the political situations and the wars that erupted.

The Glory Days of the British Empire

Top center: Queen Victoria. Top left: Officer of the 21st Lancers. Top right: Trooper in the 5th Bengali Lancers. Center: Last stand of the 24th Regiment of Foot at the Battle of Isandhlwana, Zulu War, Natal, southern Africa. Bottom left: The iron frigate HMS SHAW, with the outline of Table Mountain, Cape Town, South Africa, in the background. Bottom right: First class battleship HMS ROYAL SOVEREIGN. Behind her is outline of the Rock of Gibraltar, viewed from the southwest.

Disease was a big problem in those distant lands. Many, many British soldiers died of malaria, typhoid fever, cholera, and other diseases. (The main danger for a British soldier of the time was not war, but disease.) To maintain troop strength, shiploads of newly recruited soldiers from England were transported out to the colonies to replace the sick or dead Tommy's already on station.

TRAINING THE NEW RECRUITS

As a young cavalry officer, one of Baden-Powell's primary jobs was to train these new recruits from England and make them soldiers. When the recruits arrived in the colonies, he found them to be fairly well educated in school subjects, but they had no idea how to live out in the open. In addition, he found that they lacked the stamina for adventure, lacked bravery, and lacked self-reliance.

Baden-Powell was a still a young officer when he wrote his first two books: Reconnaissance and Scouting (1884) and Cavalry Instruction (1885). Both of these books were to be used to train new soldiers.

Baden-Powell eventually became the commanding officer of a cavalry regiment stationed in India, and was able to have a freer hand at trying out his training ideas. Several of the things he did while the colonel of the 5th Dragoon Guards are mentioned later in this book, but one is noteworthy here:

In general, he found that the more the instructor does for the soldier, the less the soldier does for himself. This does not promote self-reliance, self-confidence and bravery. Instead, it encourages the soldier to stop thinking for himself and to become dependent on his instructor.

To avoid this, Baden-Powell would often assign small groups of men ("patrols"), with no officer present, to complete a certain task. Unsupervised, and given a job to do , the soldiers had to figure out on their own how to get the job done. The more they had to solve problems for themselves and lead themselves, the more self-reliant and self-confident the soldiers became.

In addition to small groups, Baden-Powell found that an individual can learn even better. He writes…

That idea of Sir Baker Russell's of letting men make their own way to parade, etc., was acted upon by me in after years by making it imperative for every man to go a ride by himself of about one hundred and twenty miles, and to take a week in doing it. This tended to make men self-reliant, reliable, intelligent, and smart. At first it was feared that many of them, finding themselves away from all regimental restraint, would break out and make an orgy of it; but I have never heard a single complaint of the men on this head. They knew they were trusted to carry out this duty of riding off to report on some distant object, whether a railway station, a bridge, or a piece of country, and they took a pride in themselves and their horses while away, because they knew that the good name of the regiment was in their hands. We found it in practice the very best reformer for a stupid man that could be devised. He had no one to lean upon for advice or direction, he merely had his plain, simple orders, which he had to exercise his intelligence in carrying out.

This same practice I carried out also with the South African Constabulary after the Boer War. The men were generally sent out in pairs on long patrols of two to three hundred miles; but if a man were really a stupid fellow he was sent out alone. I remember well, when conducting Mr. Joseph Chamberlain on trek through the Transvaal, that we saw a solitary constable riding across the veldt. Mr. Chamberlain asked me what might be the duty of such a man, and I replied that he was probably a stupid man sent out to develop his own intelligence. We signalled the man to us and on enquiry we found that it was so. He had been ordered on a three hundred miles ride to pick up information at various spots, but with strict orders that he was not to have the help of any other constable.[1]

BROWNSEA

Baden-Powell had experience with training soldiers, but not with training boys. Before his original Scouting for Boys

---
[1] Quoted from Indian Memories, pp. 28 – 2o.

books were published, he wanted to test the ideas on real boys. He did this by holding a week long scout camp on Brownsea Island, off the coast of England. He and another adult ran the camp for 21 boys.

These boys were formed into four patrols: Ravens, Curlews, Wolves, and Bulls. The patrols acted somewhat independently, and each night one of the patrols would be sent out on bivouac.

The patrol on bivouac would pitch it's camp somewhere on the island away from the main camp. Then, until eleven o'clock at night, the patrol on bivouac would be in charge of posting sentries to catch any spies that might try to spy on their camp. The "spies" were Baden-Powell and the patrol leaders of the patrols not on bivouac.

For years, Baden-Powell had spied on and avoided some of the best warriors in the world as a scout for the British Army. However, one night at Brownsea, a young Boy Scout did what no tribal warrior or enemy soldier had ever been able to do:

A sketch of the camp at Brownsea Island

capture Baden-Powell as he spied on an enemy camp. All the Scout did was use one of the tricks that Baden-Powell had taught him.

The camp was a success, the patrol method worked as well with boys as with men, and he went ahead with Boy Scouting.

INDEPENDENCE, LOYALTY, RESPECT, AND OBEDIENCE

Baden-Powell's patrol method is a training system that teaches independence. It teaches self-reliance and self-confidence. Notice that all of these start with "self."

But the Scout Oath and Scout Law are full of words such as duty, obey, help other people, trustworthy, loyal, helpful, courteous, obedient, and reverent. A person who is independent or self-reliant, and has not learned loyalty, obedience, duty, and respect, is a menace to society. This person does not need society, and does not know how to serve society and its other members. These kind of people help populate jails and electric chairs.

BEFORE anyone learns self-reliance, that person needs to learn his duties to God, country, and others. He needs to learn obedience to authority, respect for elders, chivalry, loyalty, and reverence. If these things are not learned first, then they are more difficult to instill in a person after that person has learned to be somewhat self-confident and independent. Learning self-confidence and self-reliance is an opportunity to be able to serve others better. It is also an opportunity to hurt others better in working for self-satisfaction (another word that begins with "self".)

There is more to life than self…

THE THREE-FOLD CORD

Centuries ago, a war was taking place between the Philistines and Israelites. On one hill camped the Philistine army. Across the valley, on the other hill, camped the Israelite army, and they were afraid. Not only was the Philistine army apparently better equipped, but it had a champion: a nine foot tall giant named Goliath. Every day, morning and evening, Goliath would come down into the valley, curse Israel and their God, and challenge the Israelites to send someone out to fight him - winner take all. None of the Israelite soldiers wanted anything to do with this contest.

Then along came David, a teenage Israelite boy (note: he was the same age as a Boy Scout) who wondered why no one

Israelite officer and soldier at the front

would go down and fight Goliath. Finally, he volunteered to do it, when all of these manly soldiers would not.

Where did David get the confidence and self-reliance to be willing to do this? Was it his combat training, obedience to commanding officers, and ability to perform soldier drills? Nope. He learned it living out on his own with the sheep. He had no one to rely on but the Lord...

*"...and when a lion or a bear came and took a lamb out of the flock, *[35]*I went out after it and struck it, and delivered the lamb from its mouth; and when it arose against me, I caught it by its beard, and struck and killed it. *[36]*Your servant has killed both lion and bear; and this uncircumcised Philistine will be like one of them, seeing he has defied the armies of the living God." *[37]*Moreover David said, "The Lord, who delivered me from the paw of the lion and from the paw of the bear, He will deliver me from the hand of this Philistine." And Saul said to David, "Go, and the Lord be with you!"*

- I Samuel XVII : 34b – 37 (NKJV)

(If you want to read the rest of this story, get your Bible and read I Samuel XVII.)

Living alone in the open, and having to solve problems and face challenges, taught David to rely on the Lord. If all you have to rely on is yourself, you are missing a great deal of strength and guidance.

This scripture is not uncommonly read at weddings:

[9]*Two are better than one, because they have a good reward for their labor. *[10]*For if they fall, one will lift up his companion. But woe to him who is alone when he falls, for he has no one to help him up. *[11]*Again, if two lie down together, they will keep warm; But how can one be warm alone? *[12]*Though one may be overpowered by another, two can withstand him. And a threefold cord is not quickly broken.*

- Ecclesiastes IV: 9-12 (NKJV)

The third cord is, of course, the Lord.

Scouts have a "Duty to God," but God is not slack or lazy on His part. Don't forget His cord in your life, because it's the strongest of the three.

SUMMARY

Baden-Powell found that, whether it be army scouts or Boy Scouts, self-confidence, self-reliance, and true grit come from doing it on your own. Likewise, reliance on the Lord comes from being on your own. If, as in many organizations, the adults do all of the leading, then all the boys learn to do is follow. From the beginning, Boy Scouting has used the patrol, and the individual scout, as the method of training boys to be men, and training boy officers to lead.

CHAPTER IV

THE PATROL LEADER

Baden-Powell had many ideas on training and leadership. He was given the opportunity to put them into practice on a large scale when he took command of the 5th Dragoon Guards Regiment[1] in India. Some of his ideas involved making the regiment a better regiment by making it more skillful and proud of itself, and some of his ideas made the regiment better by getting rid of problems.

One problem that the regiment had was Enteric Fever. Men were often sick with this, and many died. He did his best to clean and sanitize the regimental housing, food supply, and water supply, but this had no effect. Finally, he decided that the men must be getting the diseases from the local market, which was anything but clean. However, since the men enjoyed going to market, it would be tough to declare it off limits. What he did instead was ask the men to avoid the market for two weeks, to see if this affected anything. The men voluntarily went along with this and, sure enough, the incidence of Enteric Fever dropped during that time.

To make the change more permanent, he provided the men with a regimental version of market, with a temperance club (and a non-temperance room for those so inclined), a bakery, dairy production and sanitation facilities, and many other distractions, all much cleaner than the market. This kept the Enteric Fevers in his regiment down.

---

[1] Dragoons (pronounced "dra-GOONS") are heavy cavalry. This is in contrast to Hussars, which are light cavalry. (By Baden-Powell's day there may not have been much of a difference between these two types of cavalry units.)

But healthy bodies are worthless if they do not do something useful. Baden-Powell found that the new recruits from England came to him with a fair amount of school knowledge, but "without individuality or strength of character, utterly without resourcefulness, initiative or the guts for adventure."[2]

A member of Baden-Powell's 5th Dragoon Guards in the field. Note the scout emblem on the sleeve.

He set about teaching the men how to scout and reconnoiter. The classes were mostly voluntary, and few attended at first. However, since the subject was not only useful to British soldiers in India but also interesting to young men, the number of attendees grew. After they had completed a course of instruction, he would put the trainees through practical tests to see how they did. Those who passed the tests were allowed to wear a badge on their sleeve in the shape of the north compass point, indicating that they were trained and accomplished scouts in the regiment. (This same compass point badge was later used as the symbol of Boy Scouting.) The men worked hard to earn it, and were proud to wear the badge. The regiment was not only better trained in this area, but the men were developing pride in their abilities as well trained soldiers.

Later, when Baden-Powell was challenged by William Smith to come up with a better system for training boys, he decided to focus on outdoor skills AND character. Baden-Powell wanted to teach boys to think, and to lead others in good directions, instead of just doing

---

[2]Quoted from Lessons from the Varsity of Life, p.272.

what everyone else is doing, or just being another "soldier." That is why the Scout Oath and Law contain so much about duty, obedience, helping others, trustworthiness, loyalty, kindness, bravery, and so on. These are all good character traits, and he hoped that you would lead others in these areas.

As a patrol leader, you have been given the opportunity to lead a patrol. It is a chance for you to try some ideas out and to see what makes a better patrol and what does not. You can work on teaching your patrol to fly high, or you can sit back and let it crawl. Will the patrol benefit greatly from your leadership, or will it just stay the same as it has always been?

*The two green bars of a patrol leader.
At times they were on a square patch, and at other times they were on a round patch. At times they have had the Scout emblem on top of them, and at other times not. At one time the bars were silver on a green patch.*

EMBLEM

The emblem, or symbol, of a patrol leader is a badge with two green bars on it. It is worn on the left sleeve, under the troop numerals.

AUTHORITY STRUCTURE OF THE BOY SCOUTS OF AMERICA

As a patrol leader you are now part of the authority structure of the BSA. You have authority over your patrol, and with that authority comes responsibility for your patrol. You are still under authority, too, and your leaders have a responsibility to you. Where do you fit in to all of this?

The basic unit of Scouting is the patrol. It has one direct leader: the patrol leader. The patrol leader has an assistant to help him.

The patrol leader answers directly to the senior patrol leader. When the patrol leader needs instructions, has a question, or has a problem, he goes to the senior patrol leader first. The senior patrol leader will also have an assistant: the assistant senior patrol leader.

The senior patrol leader answers to the scoutmaster. The scoutmaster will have assistants as well: assistant scoutmasters and junior assistant scoutmasters.

The troop committee oversees the scoutmaster. The troop committee is a group of parents and concerned adults who are the final authority in each troop. The troop committee is in charge of making sure that the troop has a good scoutmaster and that he has good assistants. They are also responsible for any major decisions that the troop as a whole might make, such as buying an expensive piece of equipment or advancing a boy in rank. You will probably not see the troop committee very often, because they do not regularly have boys attend their meetings. (If you would like to attend a troop committee meeting, ask. It is a good experience and they will allow you to be present for most committee topics.)

The troop committee answers to the sponsoring organization, which is the organization (such as a church or club) that has voluntarily adopted your troop. They usually provide a place for the troop to meet, and many of the adults in the troop are likely to be a part of the sponsoring organization. The troop committee and sponsoring organization work with the District Executive. This man is a professional, full time Scouter who watches over and works with all of the troops in his district. He will have a District Committee, made up of volunteers in the district, to help him.

The District Executive answers to the Council Executive. The Council Executive is in charge of all of the troops in his council, which is made up of several districts. He will have a Council Committee to help him. The council strip at the top of your right sleeve tells what council you belong to.

Up from there is the Area President and his Area Committee, then the Regional President and his Regional Committee. The Regional President answers to the Chief Scout Executive and his council, the National Boy Scout Council.

Each country has its own Boy Scout system of authority. In general, these different Boy Scout associations are all independent of each other, but they try to work together. There is an international Boy Scout council that coordinates many international activities.

PATROL LEADER SELECTION

Patrol leaders are selected by their patrol members, by secret ballot elections. These will usually be organized and run by the senior patrol leader at predetermined times. The term of office is generally six months to a year, and will vary from troop to troop.

The scoutmaster has the authority to nullify any patrol leader elections and to appoint leaders as he sees fit. You will find that he rarely does this, but if it should happen, do not be surprised. Sometimes, when a patrol is new, the scoutmaster will appoint the first patrol leader or two in order to get things started smoothly.

PATROL LEADER CHARACTER

The Americans were finally on the offensive against the Japanese in the Pacific. They had prevailed in the long, hard fought battle for Guadalcanal in the Solomon Islands, and were now advancing up "the Slot," an area of water that was between the two roughly parallel island chains in the Solomon Islands. The Japanese did their supply runs and ship activity at night because the American airplanes had finally taken control of the daytime skies over the Solomons. To oppose the Japanese supply and ship activity at night, the Americans sent out patrol torpedo boats, or PT boats, to find and attack Japanese ships in the dark.

On the night of August 1st and 2nd, 1943, fifteen American PT boats were patrolling the Slot looking for the four Japanese destroyers that were seen headed this way just before sunset. Some of the boats found and attacked the destroyers with no luck. The Japanese unloaded 900 men and plenty of supplies with little difficulty, and were headed back up the Slot toward Rabaul before many of the PT boats even knew they had been sighted. This meant the destroyers were approaching the PT boats from behind.

PT 109 was idling along on one engine to move quietly and save fuel when out of the darkness the Japanese destroyer AMAGIRI suddenly appeared. They were extremely close and saw each other at the same time. Commander Hanami on the AMAGIRI made a split second decision: "hard to starboard!" He rammed PT 109, cutting it in half with his ship. Gasoline from the boat was spilled into the sea and it caught fire. The rear part of the PT boat sank immediately. The front half stayed afloat. The Japanese destroyer bent her right propeller, and this was the only damage that the Japanese ships suffered all night.

Two of PT 109's crew were missing and never heard from again. The skipper, Lieutenant Kennedy, and his ten surviving crew members, stayed on the floating bow section all night and into the next day. When it looked like they were not going to be rescued, they

One end of Olasana Island, where the shipwrecked crew of PT 109 spent several days and nights. Coconuts from the palm trees provided milk for drinking, and the thick underbrush sheltered them from the sun and the Japanese.

swam three or four miles to a nearby island. Lieutenant Kennedy swam for four hours with a rope clenched in his teeth. The other end of the rope was tied to the life jacket of one of his badly injured crewmen.

Once on the island, the crew found itself in a difficult survival situation. They were on a desert island with wounded crew members and the Japanese could be anywhere. Even the natives could be unpredictable. Lieutenant Kennedy became a tremendous example of courage, endurance, and resourceful leadership to his crew while they were stranded. He also showed compassion and concern for the wounded members of his crew. He worked to keep his crew alive and to try to attract the attention of friendly forces without being seen by Japanese patrols.

They spent several nights on this and another island before being found by natives. The natives were willing to carry a message back to the PT base, and from there a PT boat came to rescue them.

Some eighteen years later, Lieutenant John F. Kennedy became the thirty-fifth president of the United States of America.

As the patrol leader, you are an example of who to be and how to be for your patrol. One of the principle criteria for electing a patrol leader should be his good moral character and his integrity. Strive to be an incredible Scout, and your patrol members will likely do the same.

The Scout Oath and Law are designed to be good guides for all Scouts. You would do well to review these and make a renewed effort to be a living example of them. We will discuss some parts of these here, especially as they relate to leadership.

Trustworthiness is extremely important. If you tell the patrol that you will check into something, or will do something, then DO IT! If the patrol begins to think that you do not do what you say, then they will stop trusting you and will stop listening to what you have to say. A leader that is ignored by his patrol cannot lead. Along the same lines, the senior patrol leader or scoutmaster may ask you to do something. If you say you will do it, DO IT! They will not trust you with responsibilities if you do not keep your word, and they will start assigning your duties (and thus your authority) to someone else.

The converse is true as well. If you cannot do a certain task, SAY SO! The patrol will continue to trust you and follow you if you are honest about your shortcomings. Also, the senior patrol leader and scoutmaster will not be let down if you were honest with them in the first place.

You must be an example of authority in action. If you cannot take orders from the senior patrol leader and the scoutmaster, how can you expect your patrol to follow your orders? You are part of an authority structure, as outlined above. Show others how to act by doing your part well, both in giving directions and in obeying directions.

Be loyal to the patrol. If you are supposed to be with them, be with them. Also, help out the members of your patrol (and other patrols) when you see the need. You will be an example of loyalty and helpfulness for your patrol to follow.

Your spirit and attitude toward things will affect the patrol greatly. If you are excited and enthusiastic, they will eventually be the same way. If you grumble and complain constantly, they will start to do that too. If you are cheerful, even when the job set before you is not fun, then the patrol will learn to be that way too. In short, your attitude will be the most important factor in influencing the patrol's attitude.

Along with this goes cleanliness. If you keep yourself clean and neat appearing, even on campouts, then the patrol will be encouraged to do the same. If you wear your uniform to meetings, the scouts will often do likewise. But another form of cleanliness is your mind and your speech. If you are a source of cuss words, dirty jokes, and dirty magazines, then your patrol will pick up these habits. If you are clean, you will be an example of cleanliness to the patrol.

A patrol leader from Scouting's younger days. Note the patrol leader's bars on his left sleeve.

Lastly, do your best. You may not succeed at everything as patrol leader, but you can be proud of your efforts IF YOU DID YOUR BEST.

PATROL LEADER RESPONSIBILITIES

Leadership starts with you. You will need to lead yourself in the direction that you want others to go. For this reason, you have the responsibility to live up to the Scout Oath and Law, and you have the responsibility to "be prepared" for whatever tasks that you know are coming up. You have the responsibility to be working on your own advancement in rank, so that you can lead others in that direction as well. You are to be an example for your patrol to follow.

The patrol is your primary responsibility beyond that. You are there to organize your patrol and to direct your patrol. You are also the first one that a Scout in your patrol is likely to come to if he has a problem or needs help. If this happens, then do your best to help the Scout. If the problem is beyond your ability, then direct the Scout to someone that can help, such as the senior patrol leader or the scoutmaster.

As the patrol leader, you will organize the patrol at the beginning of the regular troop meetings. When the command of "Fall in!" is given by the senior patrol leader, you will make sure that all of the boys line up in their proper place (usually in a line behind you). When the "sign's up," (the scoutmaster or senior patrol leader is signaling everyone to be quiet and listen by holding up the Scout Sign), then you will hold up the Scout Sign as well and have your patrol be quiet and listen to the instructions that are given.

You also direct the patrol. When instructions are given by the senior patrol leader or the scoutmaster, you direct the patrol in carrying out the instructions. If some members of the patrol are being distractive or not doing what they are supposed to be doing, you will need to get them back on track.

You are in charge of setting up and organizing patrol meetings. You can assign patrol members to help you with this. If you do not have any patrol meetings, you are to blame.

As the patrol leader you are the official representative of your patrol. You need to listen to what your patrol members

*A patrol leader keeps his patrol informed,
whether it be in person, by phone, or by mail.*

need, and what they want to do, and carry this information to the green bar meetings where events are planned. You also bring back information from these meetings and tell the patrol what is coming up in the future.

When the scoutmaster needs to have information telephoned to each member of the troop, he will call the senior patrol leader. The senior patrol leader will contact his assistant and all of the patrol leaders. The patrol leaders are responsible for contacting each member in their patrol.[3] This is how information is passed through the troop when the troop is not at a meeting.

On campouts you will be in charge of organizing food and equipment for the patrol. You may choose to have someone in your patrol do the actual organizing, but you are responsible for making sure that it gets done. You are also responsible for choosing where in the troop campsite the patrol

---

[3] A good way to do this is to call the assistant patrol leader and have him call half of the patrol members. You call the other half yourself.

will camp, and how the patrol campsite will be arranged. During competitions, you are responsible for organizing your patrol so that they will work together as a patrol in the competition. In general, if your patrol is doing something, you are the one who organizes them so that they will work together as a team: a patrol.

If the patrol does well, you will get the credit. If the patrol does poorly, you will get the blame. Whether something is officially your responsibility or not, you may want to be involved in whatever affects your patrol or its members, because eventually it may reflect on you as a leader.

APPOINTING AN ASSISTANT PATROL LEADER

The patrol leader appoints his own assistant – there is no election. As the patrol leader, you may choose any member of your patrol to be your assistant. Choose wisely!

When choosing an assistant patrol leader, look for someone with good leadership qualities. Also look for someone with good Scout skills, good character, and a good reputation. You may want to choose an assistant who is strong in an area that you are weak in, so that the two of you can complement each other.

The assistant patrol leader is not in charge of the patrol. Rather, he is there to assist you in your leadership of the patrol. However, you can delegate authority (and responsibility) to him as you need to.

THE ACTING PATROL LEADER

You are responsible to make sure that, in your absence, someone will be officially in charge of the patrol. The person who is in charge of the patrol while the patrol leader is elsewhere is called the "acting patrol leader." Usually the assistant patrol leader is the acting patrol leader when the patrol leader is gone, but if he will not be there either then you need to make sure someone is appointed to fulfill your responsibilities as patrol leader when you are not there. When you return, the acting patrol leader is to promptly step aside and let you resume your position as patrol leader, unless you tell him otherwise. He should also fill you in on what happened while you were gone.

YOUR SUCCESSOR

When your term of office is up (usually six months to a year) the senior patrol leader will hold elections. If you want to keep the job as patrol leader you can run for reelection. If you want to try a different position, then you can run for that one instead. Sometimes the scoutmaster will encourage the patrol to elect a different patrol leader so that other boys get a chance to experience that leadership position. Being a patrol leader is one of the most important ways that Scouting teaches leadership skills.

As soon as the election results are announced, the new patrol leader takes over. He appoints his assistant, who can be anyone in the patrol (including the old patrol leader or assistant patrol leader.) He should have the patrol leader patch sewn on his sleeve by the next troop meeting, and your patrol leader patch should be removed from your uniform by then.

If you are reelected as patrol leader, you can appoint the same assistant or a different one.

If you are not reelected as patrol leader, gracefully and respectfully turn over control of the patrol to the new patrol leader. If you are obnoxious and disrespectful about not being reelected, then people will not only lose respect for you but you will be showing very poor character as a Scout. At the very least, it is unlikely that anyone who sees such a negative response from a former patrol leader will ever elect him to another leadership position.

Turn control over to the new patrol leader promptly, show respect for him as your new patrol leader, and then make an effort to obey and support him as much as you wanted your patrol members to follow your instructions and support you when you were the patrol leader. Set a good example for the rest of the patrol to follow. By doing this you will still be, in a way, a leader in the patrol.

CHAPTER V

THE ASSISTANT PATROL LEADER

In June of 1940, after sweeping through Holland, Luxembourg, and Belgium, the Nazi German armies fought their way into Paris. France surrendered that same month, leaving Great Britain alone to fight the Germans. Airplanes of the German Luftwaffe began flying across the English Channel to pound England. Royal Air Force fighter pilots met them in the sky, and for a whole year the Battle of Britain raged in the skies over England.

Eventually the Germans were forced back in the air, even though they still held much of Europe on the ground. The Japanese attack on Pearl Harbor brought America into World War II, and in no time British and American planes were bombing Nazi targets in Europe.

The movie Twelve O'Clock High[1] centers around the 918th Bomber Group, United States Army Air Force. This American group flew B-17's out of Archbury, England, on raids over German occupied France. In order to try and destroy German u-boat pens, many of the raids were conducted in broad daylight at low level, which made the bombers easy targets for German fighters and German anti-aircraft gunners. Losses were high.

Colonel Keith Davenport commanded the 918th during the earlier raids. He was an excellent leader, and worked very hard. The stress and fatigue began to affect his ability to lead, though, and he was replaced as commanding officer by Brigadier General Frank Savage so that he could rest.

---

[1] Twentieth Century Fox Films, 1949.

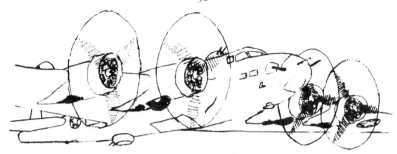

A B-17 E Flying Fortress, United States Army Air Force

When General Savage took over, he was surprised to find that the second in command had flown hardly any of the missions, even though he was one of the most experienced pilots in the group. Instead of aiding the overworked Colonel Davenport, the second in command had been dodging his responsibilities and had even been leaving base to go have fun while his commanding officer was off on missions.

The new commanding officer immediately demoted the lazy assistant to plane commander, and assigned all of the lazy and poor quality airmen to his plane. This way the deadbeat assistant could see what it was like to be a leader who needs help and have lazy people under him. He learned his lesson.

Do not be like the lazy assistant commander, and cause your patrol leader to have to do all of the work. As an assistant patrol leader you have plenty of work to do, so get busy!

EMBLEM

The emblem of the badge of office for the assistant patrol leader is a single green bar. It is worn on the left sleeve, directly underneath the troop numerals.

*The single green bar of an assistant patrol leader.
In Baden-Powell's original <u>Scouting for Boys</u> book,
the assistant patrol leader was known as the patrol corporal.*

ASSISTANT PATROL LEADER SELECTION

The assistant patrol leader is not elected but is appointed by the patrol leader. The patrol leader can appoint anyone in the patrol that he chooses, including former patrol leaders and assistant patrol leaders. Whoever is appointed as the assistant must agree to accept the job (and thus the responsibility). The APL[2] is usually selected for his helpfulness and general good character.

The patrol leader sometimes needs help, and needs someone he can rely on for that help. This is the assistant patrol leader.

HOW TO ASSIST

The assistant patrol leader is just that: an assistant. He does not have any authority over the patrol unless the patrol leader gives it to him. However, if the patrol leader is absent and has not specified who will lead the patrol while he is gone, then the assistant patrol leader becomes the acting patrol leader. The acting patrol leader has all of the authority and

---

[2]APL is the abbreviation for Assistant Patrol Leader. A list of common Boy Scout abbreviations is found in Appendix C.

responsibility of the patrol leader until the patrol leader returns. For this reason, the assistant patrol leader must know what a patrol leader is and what he does. If you skipped the last chapter on what a patrol leader is, then go back and read it; you need to know all about patrol leaders.

To assist, you are not in charge – the patrol leader is in charge. Your job is to help him do his job. If he assigns you to do something, do it. If he asks you not to do something, don't do it. If he says he needs help, help him. Sometimes he will need help but not think to ask for help. If you see something you can do to help him, ask him if he wants your help. If he says yes, do it. If he says no, don't do it.

If you see something that you can do to help the patrol leader, but he is not around to ask, then you will have to decide, to the best of your ability, if he would want you to do it or not. Whatever you decide, remember to decide by what you think HE would want, and not by what YOU want to do.

It is important for you to look for ways that you can make the patrol leader's job easier. You are there to assist him.

Often times he will ask you to do the boring part of a job so that he can be free to take care of something else. This may make you feel dumped on, but someone needs to do the boring parts. When you agreed to be the assistant patrol leader, you agreed to assist, and assisting can be a lot of boring work. But even if you become patrol leader, or senior patrol leader, or even scoutmaster, you will always be under someone's authority, and you will always have boring work to do. Many times you see the boring work that you have to do, but you do not see that the people above you have boring work to do, too. Do your work cheerfully, and you will be assisting the patrol leader more than you realize.

Much of your assisting will become indirect leadership of the patrol, as you will see…

Assistant Patrol Leader Character

Even though you are an ASSISTANT patrol leader, you are also an assistant patrol LEADER. But your leadership is not in giving directions for others to follow. Instead, it is in being an example for others to follow.

Be an example of enthusiasm and energy. You do not have to sit around and wait for the patrol leader to do something before you decide it is ok for you to do something. Take the initiative. Look for things that need to be done and do them. When the patrol leader is doing something, provide some enthusiasm for what he is doing.

If the patrol leader gives an order and you immediately complain about it, the rest of the patrol will likely do the same, and the patrol leader will have a difficult time leading. If you are grumbling or dissatisfied on a campout, the rest of the patrol will likely adopt the same attitude and the patrol will make itself miserable. On the other hand, if you are cheerful and obedient (two points of the Scout Law), even when things are rough, then things will be much more bearable, and may even turn out to be fun. Your attitude usually has a great impact on the patrol's attitude.

As an example to the patrol, be the first to do whatever you think the patrol leader would want the members of the patrol to do. Be an example of the Scout Oath and Law in action. Be prepared. Others will soon follow suit, and you will be a leader in the patrol, leading under the patrol leader's guidance.

Assistant Patrol Leader Responsibilities

The assistant patrol leader, like the patrol leader, is first responsible to make sure that he is growing and going. You should be learning Scouting skills and moving ahead in rank so that you can help others do the same. You should also be growing in the areas of the Scout Oath and Law so that you can lead others in that direction as well. Set an example by wearing your uniform proudly.

From there, your main responsibility is to the patrol leader and, through him, to the patrol. Know the patrol leader's responsibilities and look for ways to help him accomplish these. Do what the patrol leader tells you, and do it in such a way that the other members of the patrol will be enthusiastic in following the patrol leader's directions as well.

The assistant patrol leader will need to promptly take on the responsibilities of the patrol leader when the patrol leader is gone and has not appointed someone to be acting patrol leader. Be prepared to do this by knowing the patrol leader's job. When the patrol leader returns, turn over control to him quickly and tell him what he needs to know to pick up right where you are leaving off.

One of the best qualifications for leadership is knowing how to serve and how to be led. It seems easier to give orders than to take them, but if you have no experience at taking orders and at obeying, then you have no understanding of authority. Once you have experience at following, leadership will be easier because you will have a better idea of what your patrol is thinking and how to help them. Also watch how others lead. You can combine the best qualities of other leaders into your leadership when it becomes time.

CHAPTER VI

LEADERSHIP

As [Jesus] entered Capernaum, a [Roman] centurion came forward to him, beseeching him and saying, "Lord, my servant is lying paralyzed at home, in terrible distress." And [Jesus] said to him, "I will come and heal him." But the centurion answered him, "Lord, I am not worthy to have you come under my roof; but only say the word, and my servant will be healed. For I am a man under authority, with soldiers under me; and I say to one 'Go,' and he goes, and to another, 'Come,' and he comes, and to my slave, 'Do this,' and he does it."

When Jesus heard him, he marveled, and said to those who followed him, "Truly, I say to you, not even in Israel have I found such faith."

And to the centurion Jesus said, "Go; be it done for you as you have believed." And the servant was healed at that very moment.

-- Matthew VIII : 5 – 10, 13
(RSV)

This Roman centurion[1] was probably a very good and successful leader, because he showed three things that good leaders need to have. First, he understood authority. As a centurion, he had authority over many Roman soldiers, and he himself was but one officer in a Roman legion. He needed to

---

[1] A centurion is a Roman officer who has command over a Roman century, which is a group of about one hundred men. Several Roman centuries make up a Roman legion.

A Roman soldier

get his men to do the things he wanted them to do, and he himself had to do the things that his commanding officer told him to do. Likewise, you will have authority, and you will be under authority.

Second, he cared about the people under him. His whole reason for coming to Jesus was to help one of his servants who was sick. Your patrol is your responsibility, so care for the people in it.

And finally, he was humble. He did not make a big deal out of the fact that he was an officer, but instead called himself "unworthy" with regard to the honor of Jesus' presence at his house. You also should not approach your job with the attitude: "I am somebody special, so pay attention to me and show respect to me." Instead, practice ways of respecting other people and lifting them up. The way you treat others will often be the way they treat you. Show respect to them and they will start to show respect to you.

How to Be a Leader

Our current society has become quite fascinated with organizing and classifying things in order to understand and teach them. For example, we may hear about "four basic personality types," or "three main cloud types," or whatever. While there may be areas where this is useful, I believe leadership is one area where this can be harmful. When given a list of leadership styles, there is a tendency for people to think that it has to be done exactly as described, and that they have to try to use all of the styles to be an effective leader. This is NOT TRUE!

Do not view leadership as a list of a few choices where you have to pick one. Instead you can think of it as a feast. There may be several well defined dishes set out on the table, and you can pick and choose the ones that work for you. If one dish is good but has beans in it, and the beans are causing problems, then pick the beans out! Alter it to suit you. Ignore the items that don't work for you. Then, feel free to go into the kitchen and rummage around in the pantry; make your own stuff and see if it works. Go down the street to a restaurant and try what they have. Go to the store and get some stuff there. See what your dog is eating and try some of that.

In other words, you should try things and see what works best for you. Alter things as you need to to get the best results. Do not feel like you have to fit into any particular mold, and do not think that what you see is all there is.

There is no magic formula for being a leader. Sometimes what works for one person does not work for another. In general, if you will be persistent at trying to lead, you will eventually see what works and what does not. Experience is the best teacher of leadership that there is.

Here are a few suggestions for you to consider…

LEADING BY EXAMPLE

If you do not obey authority well, how can you expect your patrol to do so? If the senior patrol leader or scoutmaster tells you to do something and you do not do it, then your patrol will start to think that it is fine to ignore authority, and they will start to ignore your authority. To be a leader, be like the Roman centurion, be a good example of one who is under authority.

Also, be willing to do what you want the patrol to do. If you do not want the patrol to complain and whine, are you complaining and whining? If you want the patrol to learn about knots, are you learning about knots? If you want them to put up a dining fly, are you working on putting up the dining fly with them? If you want the patrol to be quiet and listen, are you doing the same? If you want the patrol to be living examples of the Scout Oath and Law, are you doing this? You will find that your actions speak louder than your words.

LEADING BY CRITICISM

There is a radiologist[2] that I know who gets good work out of his technicians by criticizing their work. If a technician brings him an x-ray that is not done properly, he points out what is wrong to the technician and sends the technician back to do the film over again until it is done right. After working with the radiologist for a while, the technicians learn that he will not accept poor quality films. To save time, they stop bringing the bad films to him, but simply retake the x-ray until they get it right. Then they bring only the good films to him to read.

---

[2] A radiologist is a physician who reads x-rays and does x-ray procedures. He has technicians that take many of the x-rays for him.

Now his technicians bring good films to him every time. In addition, they are proud of themselves because they are doing good work and they know it. They also respect the radiologist because he will not accept anything less than a good job.

Notice that the radiologist does not call the technicians bad or stupid, but limits himself to criticizing their work. When they do a good job, he is sure to tell them that as well, so that they are encouraged.

LEADING BY TELLING PEOPLE WHAT TO DO

Robert Baden-Powell received his first big command when he was promoted to brevet colonel and offered the command of the 5th Dragoon Guards Regiment in India. He decided to use an approach he had just learned during the Ashanti Campaign: "Softly, softly, catchee monkey."

The Ashanti tribe was a powerful tribe in the Gold Coast (the present day country of Ghana) in west Africa. When the slave trade was allowed, they would raid neighboring tribes and sell the captives as slaves. When the Europeans outlawed the slave trade, the Ashanti began to make human sacrifices out of their captives. The British told them they must stop doing this, and they refused. The British then fought them in 1874 and made them stop. When the British left, they started sacrificing people again, even though they had agreed not to. The British decided that they needed to be stopped again, so they prepared to make war with the Ashanti tribe again in 1895.

The Ashanti live inland, through thick jungles that soldiers and supplies can hardly move through. Major Baden-Powell was assigned to lead the scouting expedition ahead of the main army and to build roads and bridges through the jungle so that the main army could move quickly and easily. He and a few other white officers commanded about 500 black Africans from various tribes.

The Africans were hired, and were not eager to work. They had to cut and chop through thick jungle to make the road, and this took a lot of work. In addition, the tribesmen did not know how to tie knots and build bridges over streams and rivers, so he had to teach them. Some of the bridges would fall down when someone walked on them, and the bridge had to be rebuilt. As if this wasn't enough, the jungle was hot, wet, and full of mosquitoes, flies, snakes, and rotten

A pioneering bridge in the Gold Coast, west Africa.
If you have never been in a jungle - the air, the bugs, the foliage, and the smells can all best be described as thick.

smells. Progress was frustratingly slow, and Baden-Powell would get so impatient and mad, because he felt that his workers were lazy and did not know some of the very basics of pioneering.

However, he did not yell at them. If he made them mad at him, then they would not work harder but instead would likely quit and leave him with no workers. In addition, if he made them mad enough, the 500 negroes might turn on the whites and kill them!

Instead he used a west African proverb to calm himself: "Softly, softly, catchee monkey." When trying to catch a monkey, the hunter must be patient, and move softly. If the hunter lost his patience or made too much noise, he would likely not catch any monkeys. Likewise, if Baden-Powell lost his patience and yelled too much, he would be without any help, if not dead. He had to patiently work with his hirelings and teach them over and over how to do what he wanted them to do. It worked, and the road was built all the way to Kumasi, the Ashanti capitol. The Ashanti surrendered without a fight when the main British army arrived, and human sacrifices were stopped.

Sometimes, as patrol leader, you will need to tell someone what to do. There are several ways to do this, and some work better than others. As Baden-Powell learned quickly, getting mad and yelling at people does not usually work. Instead, people tend to oppose you when you do that, and even less will get done. The less that gets done, the more you will get mad, the more you will yell, and the less they will do. This is a bad cycle to be in.

Regardless of how upset you may be, try to keep a smile and a pleasant attitude when you tell people to do things. Saying "please" and "thank you" does much to encourage people to do what you ask.

Another trick is to ask people to do something rather than telling them to do something. "Bob, would you please pick up the trash?" usually works much better than "Bob, pick up the trash." Because teenagers can get distracted or carried away, they may not always do what you ask the first time. It's ok if you need to politely repeat your request.

There are times when asking will not work. If one or more patrol members want to do something that you know is wrong or dangerous, then tell them no. You do not have to follow the rest of the patrol in doing something that is wrong, and you should not give them permission to do this either. In the end, you are not in a good position to force them to do what you say, but you will not be blamed or get in trouble if you did your best to stop a bad situation.

LEADING BY BEING THE CAPTAIN[3]

During World War II, Japan was drawing many of its resources to wage war, especially oil, from its conquered areas in the Dutch East Indies (modern day Indonesia). Tankers and cargo ships carried these resources to Japan, in much the same way that Allied convoys carried war materials to another island nation: England. And as German u-boats were trying to cut this supply line in the Atlantic, American submarines were torpedoing Japan's ability to wage war in the Pacific, one tanker at a time.

One such undersea juggernaut was the USS WAHOO under Commander Dudley W. "Mush" Morton. Morton's leadership got results. One particular quirk of his was that he did not believe the commanding officer of a submarine should look through the periscope. He said that that caused the skipper to become focused on what he was seeing up top instead of what was happening in the boat. In other words, if you are paying attention to one captivating detail, you are ignoring other areas that you should be paying attention to.

---

[3] Sorry about that title. I couldn't think of a better and yet concise way to describe this section.

> *I like to get in and help the people I am working with, and the people that are working for me. This is generally good, but sometimes it can cause problems.*
>
> *At times past, when the ambulance would bring in a code blue (a person who is not breathing and has no heart beat – CPR is in progress), I had a tendency to help out with the IV, or help out with the airway intubation, or do the defibrillation, or get my hands on the patient and help out in some way. However, when I would do this, I usually paid so much attention to the job I was doing that I forgot to direct others on when to do things that needed to be done. For example, if I was starting a difficult IV, the defibrillations might not be as prompt as they needed to be, and I would forget to push drugs by another route until the IV was started.*
>
> *Finally, I had to get in the habit of taking my hands off of the patient, standing back where I could see everything, and then directing the resuscitation effort. When I stopped being one of the workers who became focussed on his own job, I could be "the captain" who was paying attention to the whole team and the patient as a whole. Since then my direction has been more prompt and efficient, and I am more likely to catch problems as they arise, rather than when someone finally gets my attention and points the problem out to me.*

Sometimes your job as patrol leader needs to be a job where you stand back, watch, and give directions to the individual members of your patrol. If you are doing part of the job, you may not be paying attention to the rest of the job. You are becoming a worker instead of a manager. It is ok to stand back, put your hands in your pockets, and be "the captain" when the patrol's job requires a good deal of coordination and direction.

But, just to make sure life doesn't get too easy, there will always be boys (and adults, too) that wonder why you get to be the one who stands there with his hands in his pockets telling everyone else what to do. "It's not fair! We're working and you're not!"

One good way to avoid this problem is to get in the habit of working alongside your patrol members when the task requires little or no overseeing and management. For example, if the patrol is collecting firewood, you can haul firewood too. Just remember to stop every now and then and look around – make sure everyone is doing their job, the wood pile is where you want it, and good firewood is being collected. If you are in the habit of working when the management needs are low, then when things get harder and you need to step back and supervise, the patrol will not look at you as a slacker, because you generally help out.

LEADING BY DELEGATION OF RESPONSIBILITY

If you are responsible for something, that does not mean that you have to do it all yourself. If you delegate (give) part or all of the job to someone else to do, then you are still responsible for the job and still have authority over the situation, but you are directing someone else to accomplish the job. That person answers to you just like you answer to the one who assigned you the job in the first place.

When the patrol is assigned to put up a dining fly, for example, the patrol leader is responsible for getting it done. He may assign two boys to clear off the area while another one unrolls the fly. Still other boys may be assigned to drive stakes or put up the poles. By delegating parts of the task the patrol leader is getting the job done by having everyone in the patrol do his part.

Your assistant patrol leader is a handy person to delegate some of your patrol leader jobs to. He will appreciate the trust you demonstrate for him when you give him jobs to lead in.

If you are getting overwhelmed with too much to do, it is time to delegate.

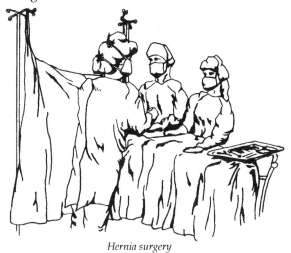
Hernia surgery

LEADING BY ORGANIZATION AND PREPARATION

The very first time that I was the surgeon instead of the assistant was in a hernia surgery. I was in residency and had assisted on a fair number of hernia surgeries before. I had also read quite a bit about the surgery and asked plenty of questions during surgery. The surgeon and I were scrubbing before the case (I was scheduled to assist) when I asked him if I could do the surgery this time.

"What makes you think you can do a hernia?" he asked.

I told him that I had assisted quite a bit (several times with this surgeon, so he knew what I was like and what I could do), and had read on the subject. I then proceeded to tell him exactly how I would do the surgery, step by step. I had worked with him enough that I knew how he liked to do the surgery, so I recited his technique back to him.

When I was done, he looked at me and didn't say anything. So I waited. We finished scrubbing and gowned. After taking our positions on opposite sides of the patient, the nurse handed him the scalpel. Instead of taking it, he pointed to me and said to the nurse, "The kid thinks he can do a hernia." She handed me the scalpel and I did it exactly as I had just described.

If you know that the patrol is going to be assigned to do something, make sure that the materials are gathered ahead of time and that you have a plan in mind for how the patrol is going to accomplish the task. The person that assigned you the task will want you to carry it out efficiently, and it is to your benefit and the patrol's benefit if you are prepared to do it efficiently. If you spend the first half hour of a project getting organized while the patrol is waiting on you, they will start to play around and lose interest. All of their attention and energy will be wasted because you were not ready.

If you are supposed to bring a list of ideas to a meeting, then get the list done ahead of time so you will be ready. You will look good and will shorten the meeting by your advanced preparation and organization. Remember, the Scout Motto is "be prepared."

CONFLICTS AND PROBLEMS

Someone in the crowd said to him, "Teacher, tell my brother to divide the inheritance with me." Jesus replied, "Man, who appointed

me a judge or an arbiter between you?" Then he said to them, "Watch out! Be on guard against all kinds of greed; a man's life does not consist in the abundance of his possessions."
- *Luke XII : 13 - 15 (NIV)*

Unfortunately, there will almost always be conflicts between people. Since you have a position of authority, many of these conflicts will become partly your responsibility. It is often tough to know what to do, and it does not get much easier as you get older. Here are some general suggestions.

Members of your patrol may not get along with each other. Many times each one will try to find someone (like the patrol leader) to take his side. The man in the above passage tried to get Jesus to take his side. Jesus not only avoided that trap, but taught the crowd a lesson at the same time. You would do well to avoid taking sides when disputes are brought to you. Instead, try to get the two people to talk to each other (instead of to others) and work things out between themselves. If you start to take sides in disputes, you will start to make problems for yourself and make enemies.

When someone does come complaining to you, their side of the story usually sounds right, and you will have a tendency to assume that the other person is in the wrong. However, usually the first side of a story you hear will sound right. It is important to go and get the other side of the argument before making any decisions, or I guarantee you will make yourself look stupid.

If two members of your patrol are constantly fighting and not getting along, and you are not having any success at working with them, you can talk to your senior patrol leader or scoutmaster about the situation.

If there is a problem between you and a member of your patrol, you will need to continue your duties as patrol leader regardless of how you feel. Try to talk with the person privately and see if the two of you can work things out. Do NOT complain about that person to other members of the patrol, as this will only encourage people to take sides and will create a lot of hard feelings. It is also more difficult for you to come to peaceable terms with someone that you are having problems with if he hears that you have been spreading bad things about him. If you are making no progress, talk to the senior patrol leader or the scoutmaster about the situation.

This goes for losing your temper as well. As Baden-Powell said, "Never lose your temper with him. If you are in the right there is no need to, and if you are in the wrong you can't afford to.[4]"

If you are having problems with someone in authority over you, such as the senior patrol leader or an assistant scoutmaster, then try to work it out between the two of you. If you cannot come to a good understanding, then talk with the scoutmaster. Again, do not speak badly about these people to others.

Lastly, if you are having problems with the scoutmaster, try to work it out with him. If this can't be done, then you may need to talk to your parents or the troop committee chairman.

SUCCESS

Success is when you win! Success is when you accomplish what you meant to, or better yet, when you accomplish more than you meant to.

Success breeds confidence. Confidence breeds aggressiveness and a willingness to try new things. Confidence, aggressiveness, and a willingness to try new things usually leads to more success. See the cycle?

---

[4] From Lessons from the Varsity of Life, p. 315.

Failure breaks this up. Failure destroys confidence, which can lead to timidity and a reluctance to try new things. Failure seems to be the enemy of success.

That is why some children's games these days have no winner and no loser. I was at a youth baseball game not too long ago. When I asked who won, I was informed that there are no longer winners and losers. Losing is failure, and who wants their child to feel failure?

Life is not like that. Life is about being a bread winner or losing a job. Life is about passing a class or failing a class. Leading a patrol is about succeeding at getting them to do what you want them to do, or failing at getting them to do what you want them to do. Somewhere along the line, you need to learn how to deal with failure, or else when you start to fail, you will think that YOU are the failure...

FAILURE

When my wife and I were first dating, we were out in the woods one evening, and she expressed a desire to have some hot chocolate.

Hot chocolate? No problem! So I set about building a fire to heat the water on. I did not do so well with the first match, and the fire started with the second match soon died as well. The third match was the one that did the trick, and in no time I had water warming over the fire. I felt a little annoyed at having so much of a problem with the fire, but at least that was behind me.

When the water was finally boiling she was ready for the hot chocolate. Instead of smoothly retrieving the boiling water I managed to spill it on the fire, completely dousing the fire and leaving me with nothing but soaking wet ashes to work with! My girlfriend looked at me and said, "I thought you were an Eagle Scout!"

So after feeling rotten, I started all over again with the fire. This time I was successful.

However, my girlfriend's family sure poked fun at me for a while about this. My future sister in law even gave me a book of matches that was over a foot long! On it she wrote, " <u>PLENTY</u> of matches... (just in case you can't get a fire going after the first hundred tries or so.)"

When you try your hand at leadership, I guarantee you will fail at times. Boys in your age group can be very hard on a person that fails, and this can make things even worse. You may be laughed at, teased, pushed aside, or who knows what else.

As a boy leader, the adult leaders will expect you to fail every now and then. They want to build experience and confidence in your ability to lead, so they will give you more chances to try again than you may think you want. Don't give up, keep at it.

The boys can be rough on you for a short while, but they will soon move on to something else. Usually it is the person that fails that has the most anxiety about trying again. It is acceptable to be afraid or anxious, but you will still need to conquer these feelings and try again. Leadership and confidence come with experience. Don't give up without getting the experience you need.

When I was in training, I made a remark to an attending physician (teacher) one day that he had some really good advice on a difficult patient. He replied, "Good judgement comes from experience, and experience comes from poor judgement!" The people around you that seem to never fail have already failed enough times to know what to do and what to avoid. You are going through the same process.

Sometimes the failure is all your fault. This does not change your need to try again. You do need to learn from your mistakes and keep trying, or your mistakes will stop you from having success.

Whether the failure is your fault or not, there are some other feelings you may have to deal with…

PAIN AND GUILT

Dr. Paul Brand was, at one point in his life, a missionary physician in India. He became interested in leprosy and worked with people so afflicted.

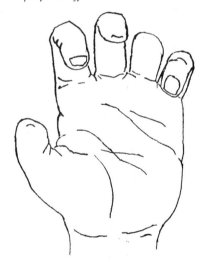

Missing digits and claw hand deformity characteristic of leprosy

Leprosy causes many physical damages which disfigure a person. The fingers will partially fall off, leaving stubs where there used to be fingers. Also, what is left of the fingers tends to become permanently turned inward, making the hand look like a claw. The toes often are missing on the feet, and the feet themselves can be quite deformed. The nose caves in, leaving a flat, odd looking face where there was once a pretty face. Lepers will often have large, open sores on their hands or feet, which ooze puss or blood. All of these things make lepers outcasts from most societies.

As he was studying leprosy, Dr. Brand learned that many of the lepers could not feel things in their hands and feet. They would injure themselves and not know it.

One day, while visiting a leprosarium in southern India, he saw several lepers running to greet him. One was a boy who had bandages on his foot and was using crutches to hobble along. Needless to say, the people without crutches were able to outrun him, so he was left behind. This frustrated him, so he stopped using the crutches and ran to catch up with the others. When he started running on his injured foot, it tore mostly off, so that he ended up running on the bloody, exposed bone end of his leg. He finally ran up to Dr. Brand, panting and smiling because he had made it so quickly. Dr. Brand and the other people working at the hospital were horrified because the boy had almost completely torn his foot off, but the boy did not even feel it. The boy's foot and lower leg had to be amputated.

Dr. Brand had been suspecting that most of the deformities and sores of leprosy were caused by the patient's lack of pain. If a leper injured himself, he could not feel it and would not take care of the injury. It would get worse, become infected, and soon the person would lose a finger, a toe, a hand, a foot, or develop a deformity or sore that would not heal. As it turns out, he was right.

God gave you such unpleasant things as pain and guilt so that you will know when something is wrong. If you do not know about a problem, then you cannot fix the problem. If you stub your toe, the pain in your toe will tell you that it is injured, so that you will know to be careful with it and take care of it. If you do something and then feel guilty, your conscience is letting you know that there is a problem that needs to be dealt with. Woe to the person who has no pain fibers or no conscience! The former hurt themselves, the latter hurt others.

There are some medical diseases that cause pain inappropriately, and sometimes we have learned to feel guilty over something that we do not need to feel guilty for. But by and large, pain and guilt are warning you, and you need to listen.

Some people will ignore pain and guilt. You can do this, but this does not get rid of the problem. Instead, the feelings fester, and you will be worse off in the end, as will the people around you.

Some people will tell their side of the story over and over to various people, hoping to find someone that will justify what they did. If you do this, eventually you will find someone who will tell you that you did not do anything wrong, so you don't need to feel guilty. But there is always someone out there that will agree with you, no matter how wrong you may be. Just because you find someone else to justify you does not mean that you are right.

Another way that people avoid dealing with guilt is to divert the attention away from the problem. They may blame someone else, or blame the situation. Sometimes they will point out some of the good things they have done, drawing attention away from the mistake. But none of these fixes the problem.

If you did something wrong, go and apologize. If you hurt someone, then let them know that you are sorry. If you messed up, admit it.

When you have done this, and done your best to repair any damage you have done, then you have only one more thing to do: do your best to avoid the same mistake in the future. Once you have done all of this, you no longer need to feel guilty – you have done all that you can.

UNPLEASANT TASKS

No matter who you are or where you go in life, there will always be jobs to do that are no fun. As a matter of fact, some jobs may be downright unpleasant, disgusting, or painful.

Baden-Powell once pointed out that the longer and longer you spend looking at an unpleasant task, the worse and worse it will look. Instead, he suggested going at it boldly and getting it done. It generally does not look nearly so bad once you have begun.

If a task has been assigned to you, do your best to get it done. You can go one better by having a good and cheerful attitude while working on it. People will be impressed and the task will go better.

Charles Swindoll once said: "I am convinced that life is 10% what happens to me and 90% how I react to it."[5]

(Go back and read that last sentence again. If you learn that, and make an effort to control your attitude, you just became a better person, and your life just became a whole lot more pleasant.)

And now, after you have read this whole chapter on leadership, I have some bad news for you: You cannot learn leadership from a book! You learn to lead by leading. You learn to lead by trying, and succeeding, and failing; all of these teach you what works and what does not work for you. Your strong efforts, your successes, your failures, your experiences, and your attitude, will teach you leadership like no book can ever do.

---

[5] Original reference unknown. I found this in a photocopy that did not give a reference.

CHAPTER VII

PATROL MEETINGS AND ACTIVITIES

When I was a patrol leader, I did not even know that we could have patrol meetings, much less have any idea on how to run a patrol meeting. I thought Scouting consisted of troop activities, and that the patrol was a convenient way to group boys for troop purposes. I never read any books on how to be a patrol leader, and I never asked anyone how to be a patrol leader. My patrol never had one single patrol meeting, because I never called one. I hope you and your patrol will not be like that.

I had a good time in Scouts, and learned quite a bit. My troop was an active and interesting troop. Every now and then I hear a Scout complain that Scouts is boring, or that their troop does not do anything. If you think that your troop is boring or not very active, and you are a patrol leader, then it is your fault, because you are in a position to do something about it.

PATROL MEETINGS

A patrol meeting can be conducted just about however you want it to be. There is no set way to run a patrol meeting. You may have noticed that your troop meetings are not run the same way every time, and patrol meetings do not need to be the same every time either. If you are short on ideas on how to run a patrol meeting, look at your troop meetings to get some ideas. I will also give you some ideas here.

The Scout Motto is "Be Prepared." Before you ever start a patrol meeting, be prepared by deciding what you are going to do at the patrol meeting. Collect any materials and help that you may need ahead of time.

Patrol meetings can generally (but not always) follow the format of: Opening, Announcements, Activity, Plan for the next patrol meeting, and Closing. You can alter these as you want to see what works best for you and your patrol.

OPENING: This is the official start of the meeting. It can be one or more of the following: your patrol yell, the Pledge of Allegiance, the Scout Oath, the Scout Law, the Scout Motto, the Scout Slogan, and prayer. This tells everyone to be quiet and pay attention because the meeting has started.

ANNOUNCEMENTS: If the patrol leader or any one else has any information that needs to be shared with the rest of the patrol, this is a good time to do it.

ACTIVITY: This is the main part of the meeting. Whatever the patrol got together to do is the activity. Maybe the patrol got together to play Capture the Flag, or to go swimming, or to track and stalk animals in some nearby woods, or to learn about maps and compasses, or to learn some first aid, or to do just about anything else you can think of.

If there is someone who is going to teach, whether it be an adult that you invited to the meeting or a member of the patrol, then turn the meeting over to that person to lead the teaching. If you got together to tour a fire hall, or an ambulance barn, or an airport, or wherever, then turn the meeting over to the guide at that place. As the patrol leader or assistant, you should not interrupt the person who is teaching or guiding, but instead help keep the patrol paying attention.

PLAN the next patrol meeting: When the activity is done, spend some time deciding what you all want to do for the next patrol meeting. Decide whom you may need to contact to help with the meeting. Decide when and where the meeting will be held. This way, everyone gets a voice in what the patrol is doing and everyone knows when and where to go for the next patrol meeting.

CLOSING: The closing officially ends the meeting. It can be prayer, patrol yell, the Scout Oath, Law, Motto, or Slogan, the Pledge of Allegiance, or any combination of these. It can also be something else, if you prefer.

PATROL ACTIVITIES

Patrol activities are similar to patrol meetings, but may last longer than a typical meeting. Patrols can plan a hike or a campout, and do this as a patrol activity. Maybe the patrol wants to go fishing or swimming all day, or maybe they want to play Capture the Flag or some other game all afternoon. Perhaps they want to spend the day at the beach, or the rifle range, or doing volunteer work. A patrol can do just about anything for an activity that its members can dream up.

Most patrol activities are purely activity. There can be an opening, some announcements, a closing, and all of that kind of stuff, but there does not usually need to be.

When I lived in West Africa, we would always start our trips out with prayer. Since I was not accustomed to doing this, it was a little different at first. However, after seeing what traveling in West Africa was like, I was glad that we started our trips out that way. If you want to start your activities out with something, I think prayer is a good idea.

WHO TO INVITE TO A PATROL MEETING

The people that should always be invited to every patrol meeting are the patrol members. Even if there may be some members that you like less than others, it is not a patrol meeting unless the ENTIRE patrol is invited.

Also, you will need to have at least one adult present. If you are meeting at someone's house, this is usually not a problem. As long as there is an adult home when you have the meeting, you have an adult available. Incidentally, the parents of each patrol member should know where the patrol meeting will be, what you will be doing, and when you will be done.

Lastly, if you need to invite someone to come and teach the patrol something, be sure to invite that person. You can invite anyone to come and teach the patrol something, including scoutmasters, parents, troop committee members, police officers, or whoever you think you may want to invite.

BUT I CAN'T DO IT

As a patrol leader, there will be many things that you are not able to do by yourself. You may have some great ideas, but you may find yourself unable to do anything about these ideas.

If you need help, get it. Ask people that can help to help. If you are turned down by the first person you ask, try someone else. If that person turns you down too, try a third person. Ask members of the patrol for help, or ask patrol members if their dads can help. Ask the scoutmaster or one of his assistants for help. If you need help, be persistent at finding someone to help, and eventually you will find someone. You are not expected to do everything by yourself.

If an adult tells you that you should not carry out your plans because it is wrong or dangerous, then you need to find something else to do. But if the only problem is finding help, then check around until you find the help you need.

CHAPTER VIII

PATROL MEMBERSHIP

Airplanes have made world travel so much faster and easier these days. But even with advancing technology, people are still the same. Living in or visiting another country lets you see this, and you can start to see this before you even leave the airport. One interesting airport is Lagos International Airport in Nigeria, west Africa.

Although many of the people in the airport are good people, there are many who are not. Many of the workers regard white[1] people as people to make money off of, so they will invent ways of doing this. For example, when you are going through customs to enter Nigeria, and they find you are carrying something valuable, they will sometimes tell you about a "Nigerian law" (that does not really exist, but since you cannot prove it, you cannot argue with them about this) that this item cannot be brought into the country without special paperwork. What this means is that you cannot take it into the country, and usually you cannot send it back on the plane for one reason or another. You will have to let them keep the expensive item at the airport until they can process whatever "special paperwork" that they have to do to clear it. So you leave it at customs and, the next time you check on it, you are told that it has "disappeared." They will let you know when they find it, which they never do. A dishonest customs official has taken it home or sold it.

---

[1] Although whites are the common targets, American blacks are taken advantage of as well, even though they often do not expect to be taken advantage of by Africans. But to the Africans an American is an American, regardless of skin color.

A Nigerian one naira coin.
In 1973 it was worth about $1.50.
In 1996 it was worth a little over 1¢

Another trick is seen when you leave the country and are going through customs. The dishonest customs official will go through your luggage and find something that you bought in Nigeria (and most people buy something in Nigeria). He will then say something like "Do you have papers to show that this is not a national treasure or artifact? It is illegal to take such out of the country." What are you going to do? In reality, no such paperwork exists, but you cannot win an argument with a customs official over Nigerian law. Your plane will leave soon and he is going to make you miss your plane by not passing you through customs. After a few moments to let you realize the dilemma you are in, he will be "helpful" by suggesting that if you give him a little money he will look the other way and let you go through.

At this point, if you look up, you will see a red sign directly over the customs official's head, that says "Give no bribe." This has been such a problem that the airport has had to put up signs, but the signs do not seem to help.

If you come into the country another way, such as by car, it is even worse. There will be police road blocks set up every few miles, and some of the police will make sure that they find some "law" that you are breaking. However, they repeatedly remind you that if you will give them a little something (i.e. – a bribe) they will let you go on. Then you get to the next police roadblock and the same thing happens again. Once you get a good ways past the border this lets up, and the police roadblocks become a nuisance instead of a never ending string of bribe requests.

It was difficult for us to get through all of this, especially since myself and the people I was working with refused to be dishonest and bribe Nigerian government officials. I spent plenty of time going nowhere while a crooked government worker was waiting for me to bribe him.

The market is not much better. One (white) friend of mine was walking along when a Nigerian came up to him and offered to sell him a straw hat for 2,000 naira (about $25). My friend looked at him and said, "Why should I buy this hat from you when I can buy the same hat in a nearby town for only forty naira?" (about 50 cents.) The Nigerian man looked astonished and said, "Oh, you are not a tourist???" He then went on to look for some other "tourist" to sell the hat to.

If all people in Nigeria were like that, we would never go back. However, one Nigerian passport agent stands out in my mind as being the opposite. When my wife and I arrived, it was a very hot and humid day, and we were last in line. The passport agent informed us that my wife could get out of line and pass through, so that she could sit down and rest. I was to wait in line and check us both in when I finally had my turn at the booth. For those of you who don't know, that is an example of chivalry; old Boy Scout Handbooks have a chapter on chivalry. I appreciated the chivalrous treatment my wife received.

We met many other good people in Nigeria, and some of them went out of their way to be helpful and to make us feel welcome. These people are the ones who made this new place much more like a home while we were there, and these are the people that I have the warmest memories of.

Helping the new person feel welcome is very important if you want the new person to stay. You were new to Scouting once, and can think of things that you wish people had told you about or had done for you. Try doing these for the new Scout.

GETTING NEW MEMBERS

When a boy joins the troop he will be assigned to a patrol. This is usually a scary time for the newcomer, because he may not know most of the other boys and, since boys tend to join Scouts at a younger age, most of the boys in the troop will be older and bigger than him. Instead of showing him who's boss, be nice to him and make him feel welcome. Show him what to do, and let him know what is happening, or why we are doing this or that. This boy may be the one who will lead your patrol in the future. Would you want him to remember you as a helpful, selfless person or a greedy "customs official." People will know what you are like by what you do.

LOSING MEMBERS

Sometimes boys are transferred to a different patrol by the scoutmaster. If this happens, do not treat the boy badly; he is a former patrol member and still a fellow scout.

Sometimes a patrol loses a member because the member stops showing up. If one of your patrol members hasn't been to a meeting for a while, call him and find out why. Does he need a ride? Are the regular meeting nights bad for him? Is he mad at somebody? Find out what the problem is and do your best to fix it.

GETTING RID OF MEMBERS

If there is a boy in the patrol who is continually causing problems, first talk to him about this and see what can be done.

If this has failed, talk to the senior patrol leader or scoutmaster. If it is during a patrol meeting, you can ask him to leave, but you do NOT have the authority to kick someone out of Scouts. sometimes a boy who is more interested in causing problems than in participating in Scouts will be dismissed from the troop, but this is done by the scoutmaster, not by you.

Your goal should not be to get rid of troublemakers, but to try to get them to be better Scouts. Getting rid of someone is a last resort.

CHAPTER IX

PATROL RECORDS

Elephants have been used for many centuries and in many ways in India. One elephant, about a hundred years ago, was condemned to wear heavy chain bracelets around each of his ankles because he had killed several people one day.

This elephant was carrying British Army tents as a pack on his back and wading across a river. He began to feel his feet sinking in the sand and mud on the bottom of the river. Walking next to him were several natives, so he reached out with his trunk and grabbed one. He pushed the native under the river's surface and stuffed him under a foot that was sinking in the mire. This gave the elephant a better foothold.

Seeing that this helped, the elephant snatched up another nearby native with his trunk and pushed him under another foot. He did this with two or three natives.

As you may guess, having an elephant push someone into the mud on the bottom of a river and then stand on him will kill him, and this is how the elephant killed several unfortunate natives one day.[1]

This story is a true story, but it happened so long ago that all of the people who saw this happen are dead, including the elephant. If Baden-Powell had not written this story down, we would never know that it happened.

---

[1] This is from pages 36-37 of <u>An Old Wolf's Favourites</u>, by Robert Baden-Powell.

WHY KEEP RECORDS?

There are three main reasons why you would want to keep patrol records. The first is to answer questions that may arise in the future. Was John ever a member of the Owl Patrol? Did Andrew go on the last campout? (This is handy information when it comes time to satisfy camping requirements for advancing in rank.) Who was the patrol patrol leader of the Rattlesnake Patrol two years ago? Did Jim bring his part of money for the new patrol flag? If records are kept, then these and other types of questions that may arise in the future can be answered without guesswork or arguing.

An Indian pack elephant

Secondly, it is sometimes fun to review what the patrol has done and who has been involved. Many of the stories in this book would not be here if someone had not written them down a long time ago. If the patrol has records, then these can be enjoyed by anyone, including yourself, for as long as the records exist.

Lastly, keeping patrol records teaches you how to keep records. What is important to write down and what is not? How do you store records? How do you find information in the records? Someday you may be the secretary of an organization. Now is a good time to learn how to keep records.

WHO KEEPS THE RECORDS?

The responsibility begins with the patrol leader, but he can delegate this to someone else in the patrol if he chooses. Whoever keeps the records should be reliable to keep them up to date and reliable not to lose them.

Often times the patrol records are stored with the troop records at the regular troop meeting place so that they will be available for the troop meetings. If the records go home with someone, be sure that that person brings the records back next week.

PATROL MEMBERSHIP RECORDS

From the time a patrol is formed, the names of the boys in the patrol should be written down, along with when they joined the patrol (month and year.) Also keep the boy's address and telephone number, so he can be contacted at home if need be.

A continuous list of all of the boys in the patrol should be kept. When someone leaves the patrol, do not "erase" his name, but simply write down the date that he "graduated" or left, whichever the case may be.

PATROL ACTIVITY RECORDS

When the patrol goes on any activity, whether it be a troop campout or a patrol hike, the date(s) should be written down as well as what the activity was. Also include a list of all of the boys who went, and who was the patrol leader (or acting patrol leader) for the trip. Lastly, keep track of who paid for their part of the trip (food, gasoline, etc.) and who did not.

PATROL FINANCE RECORDS

Money records are important because money can be a contentious issue. Any time that a boy contributes money for a patrol activity, the boy's name, the date, and the amount of money should be written down. For campouts, the members of a patrol usually split the cost of the food and other expenses evenly. Keep track of who has paid their share and who has not. If you want to follow good business practice, you should give a receipt every time someone pays. However, for the patrol, a receipt is usually not necessary as long as it is written in the patrol records.

CHAPTER X

DISBANDING THE PATROL

As the boys of a patrol work together and advance, they will eventually become Eagle Scouts. Regardless of rank, boys continue to grow in age as well, and at the age of eighteen a boy is no longer eligible to be in a patrol. When he reaches that age, if he still wants to be active in Scouting, he becomes an assistant scoutmaster.

Usually a scoutmaster will allow the boys in a patrol to "graduate," and will not refill the patrol with new boys. Instead he is likely to start a new patrol with the new boys so that they have a patrol to build and be proud of during their time in Scouting. This does not mean that your patrol is no longer any good. On the contrary, it means that the patrol has completed its task and is ready to be retired. This is both a happy time and a sad time. It is sad to see a patrol end, but it is also exciting to look back and see how much the patrol did together, and how much they accomplished.

A patrol will have some items to take care of. The patrol flag usually is given to the last person to be the patrol leader. If he does not want it or is not likely to preserve it, then someone else in the patrol should keep it. The patrol records usually go with the patrol flag.

Any patrol equipment can be divided among the patrol members at the time that the patrol is disbanded. If they want, they can donate the patrol equipment to the troop. Keep in mind that if the troop purchased the patrol equipment then the equipment belongs to the troop and cannot be divided up among the patrol members. Only equipment bought by the patrol, independent of the troop, can be done with as the patrol wishes.

Any patrol money should be given to the troop.

By the time a patrol has been in existence for many years, there is much to look back on, and many good memories. Even after your patrol is no longer an active part of Scouting, the memories and the friendships will make it so your patrol will never cease to exist.

The Boy Is There No More

The cannon smoke, the lofty sail,
    The clash of pirate sabers,
The hero comes, the damsel saved,
    What fun, this boyhood labor!
But dreams give way, as day by day,
    The sands of pirate shores,
Hold less the time, and soon we find,
    The boy is there no more.

The lion roars, the bear, he waits,
    To wrestle the lad again,
And though they've lost so many times,
    Why should the good times end?
But backyard jungles, and alley seas,
    Cannot survive alone,
Youth fans their life, where can he be?
    The boy is there no more.

The chest grows deep, the toys, they sleep,
    Who can halt the rising years?
Father, where is that boy of yours?
    And mother, why the tears?
The Lord well knows, and teaches souls,
    That brawn makes not a man,
For all boys grow, so take the time,
    To teach them while you can.

The heart of God, the love of life,
    A heed to duty's call,
An honest tongue, a cheerful smile,
    Make big and strong and tall.
Where is the boy? We hope to find,
    That he is there no more;
For in his place, there stands a man,
    Who was but a boy before.

Author's Patrols

Frontiersman Patrol
(Scout)
Troop 144
Central Wyoming Council

Fox Patrol
(Wood Badge)
W5-638-97
Central Wyoming Council

BIBLIOGRAPHY

Baden-Powell, Sir Robert S.S.: B.- P.'s Outlook. National Council, Boy Scouts of Canada, Canada. 1979. (This book is a reprint of a book of the same title first published in 1941, and is a collection of his comments written for "The Scouter" magazine from 1909 to 1941.)

Baden-Powell, Bvt. Lieutenant-Colonel Robert S.S.: The Downfall of Prempeh. Methuen & Co., England. 1896. (Reprinted by Stevens Publishing Co., Kila, Montana, USA.)

Baden-Powell, Sir Robert S.S.: Indian Memories. Herbert Jenkins Limited, London, England. 1915.

Baden-Powell, Lord Robert S.S.: Lessons from the Varsity of Life. 1933. (Reprinted by Stevens Publishing Company, Kila, Montana, USA.)

Baden-Powell, Sir Robert S.S.: An Old Wolf's Favourites. J.B. Lippincott Co., Philadelphia, Pennsylvania, USA. 1922.

Beach, Commander Edward L.: Submarine! Henry Holt and Co., New York, New York, USA. (1952 printing) 1946.

Birchard, C. C.: Boy Scout Songbook. Edited and published by Boy Scouts of America, Massachusetts, USA. (1920?)

Boy Scouts of America: Junior Leader Handbook. Boy Scouts of America, Irving, Texas, USA. (1996 printing) 1990.

Boy Scouts of America: The Official Patrol Leader Handbook. (Third Ed., Second Printing) Boy Scouts of America, Irving, Texas, USA. 1980.

Brand, Paul, and Philip Yancy: Pain: The Gift Nobody Wants. HarperCollins Publishers, New York, New York, USA. 1993.

Bryan, Roy: Scout Officer Training Course. (Unpublished.)

Donovan, Robert J.: PT 109: John F. Kennedy in World War II. McGraw-Hill Book Company, Inc., New York, New York, USA. 1961.

Freedman, Russel: Scouting with Baden-Powell. Holiday House Inc., New York, New York, USA. 1967.

Falls, Cyril: The Great War. Capricorn Books, New York, New York, USA. 1959.

Hillcourt, William, with Olave, Lady Baden-Powell: Baden-Powell, The Two Lives of a Hero. G.P. Putnam's Sons, New York, New York, USA. 1964.

Keating, Bern: PT Boats in World War II... The Mosquito Fleet. Scholastic Book Services (by arrangement with G.P. Putnam's Sons), New York, New York, USA. (1966 printing), 1963.

Mason, Herbert Molloy, Jr.: The Great Pursuit. Random house, Inc., New York, New York, USA. 1970.

Preston, Antony: Cruisers, An Illustrated History 1880 – 1980. Bison Books Ltd., London, United Kingdom. 1980.

Tompkins, Frank: Chasing Villa. The Military Service Publishing Co., Harrisburg, Pennsylvania, USA. 1934.

Tuchman, Barbara W.: The Guns of August. McMillan Company, New York, New York, USA. 1962.

Upton, Bvt. Major-General Emory: Infantry Tactics, Double and Single Rank, Adapted to American Topography and Improved Fire-arms (Revised Ed.) D. Appleton and Company, New York, New York, USA. 1883.

Appendix A

Patrol Patches (and Names) Available from the BSA, 1998

Alligator	Lightning
Antelope	Moose
Badger	Owl
Bat	Panther
Bear	Pedro (donkey)
Beaver	Pheasant
Bison (Buffalo)	Pine Tree
Bobcat	Raccoon
Bobwhite	Ram
Cobra	Rattlesnake
Dragon	Raven
Eagle	Roadrunner
Flaming Arrow	Scorpion
Flying Eagle	Shark
Fox	Stag (deer)
Frog	Tiger
Frontiersman	Viking
Hawk	Wolf
Indian	Wolverine
Liberty (bell)	(blank)

Appendix B

Baden-Powell Patrol Requirements

The Baden-Powell Patrol Award is given to patrols who demonstrate that they are an outstanding patrol by completing the requirements listed below. The award itself is a patch with a star that is worn under the patrol emblem on the left sleeve. The requirements take at least three months to complete.

1. **Show patrol spirit** by using and rallying around your patrol flag. Demonstrate and use your patrol yell and patrol call. Keep your patrol records accurate and current for at least three months. Put your patrol symbol on your equipment.

2. **Patrol meetings** must be held for at least three months, with at least two meetings per month.

3. **Participate**, as a patrol, in at least one outdoor activity or event in a three month period of time.

4. **Do two service projects** in a three month time period. These projects must be approved ahead of time by the Green Bar Council (Patrol Leader's Council.)

5. **Show advancement in rank** by having two patrol members go up at least one rank in three months.

6. **Uniforms** must be up to date and worn by at least six Scouts in the patrol.

7. **At Green Bar (Patrol Leader's Council) meetings**, the patrol must be represented by the patrol leader or his designee, at least three times in three months.

Appendix C

Some Common Abbreviations Used In Scouting

APL	Assistant Patrol Leader
ASM (or SA)	Assistant Scoutmaster
ASPL	Assistant Senior Patrol Leader
BSA	Boy Scouts of America
JASM	Junior Assistant Scoutmaster
PL	Patrol Leader
QM	Quartermaster
SM	Scoutmaster
SPL	Senior Patrol Leader

Appendix D

Camp Bugle Calls

At many Scout camps the bugle will be used. This appendix is to help you recognize the bugle calls and know what they are for. A brief description follows each one.

CALLS FOR THE DAILY ROUTINE:

First Call

This is also called Assembly of Trumpeters, and calls the buglers together first thing in the morning. If the camp only has one bugler, then this is often not played. It also serves as a preliminary wake up call for the camp.

Reveille

This is the wake up call for the camp. Everyone should be getting up when it is done.

Assembly

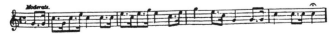

When this is played, the camp assembles at the main meeting area for the camp (usually the parade grounds.)

Mess

Played when a meal is ready and people are supposed to assemble together to eat. This is frequently omitted, especially if meals are at regular times or if the camp is already assembled just prior to meal time.

Tattoo

Sounded at the end of the day. This is the call for the camp to enter their tents and shut the doors of their tents in preparation for going to sleep. It is omitted at many camps.

Taps

Played as the last call of the day. It is also called Extinguish Lights, and means that the camp is to turn out the lights in the tents and go to sleep.

CALLS FOR THE FLAG:

To The Color

Played when the flag is being raised in the morning.

Retreat

Played when the flag is lowered in the evening.

OTHER CALLS:

Officer's Call

Calls the officers (Green Bar) together for a meeting.

Charge

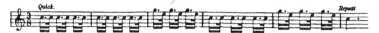

This is included just for fun. Charge!

EXAMPLE OF A TYPICAL DAY USING BUGLE CALLS

6:45 am	**First Call**
7:00 am	**Reveille**
8:00 am	**Assembly**
	To The Color – for morning flag ceremony
	Breakfast (Mess not played because the camp is already assembled.)
Noon	**Mess** – for lunch
5:00 pm	**Assembly**
	Retreat – for evening flag ceremony
	Supper (Mess not played because the camp is already assembled.)
10:00 pm	**Tattoo**
11:00 pm	**Taps**